Exceedingly
Growing
FAITH

Exceedingly Growing FAITH

By Kenneth E. Hagin

Unless otherwise indicated, all Scripture quotations in this volume are from the *King James Version* of the Bible.

Second Edition
Eighth Printing 1995

ISBN 0-89276-506-2

<table>
<tr><td>

In the U.S. write:
Kenneth Hagin Ministries
P.O. Box 50126
Tulsa, OK 74150-0126
</td><td>

In Canada write:
Kenneth Hagin Ministries
P.O. Box 335, Station D,
Etobicoke (Toronto), Ontario
Canada, M9A 4X3
</td></tr>
</table>

BOOKS BY KENNETH E. HAGIN

* Redeemed From Poverty, Sickness and Spiritual Death
* What Faith Is
* Seven Vital Steps To Receiving the Holy Spirit
* Right and Wrong Thinking
  Prayer Secrets
* Authority of the Believer (foreign only)
* How To Turn Your Faith Loose
  The Key to Scriptural Healing
  Praying To Get Results
  The Present-Day Ministry of Jesus Christ
  The Gift of Prophecy
  Healing Belongs to Us
  The Real Faith
  How You Can Know the Will of God
  Man on Three Dimensions
  The Human Spirit
  Turning Hopeless Situations Around
  Casting Your Cares Upon the Lord
  Seven Steps for Judging Prophecy
* The Interceding Christian
  Faith Food for Autumn
* Faith Food for Winter
  Faith Food for Spring
  Faith Food for Summer
* New Thresholds of Faith
* Prevailing Prayer to Peace
* Concerning Spiritual Gifts
  Bible Faith Study Course
  Bible Prayer Study Course
  The Holy Spirit and His Gifts
* The Ministry Gifts (Study Guide)
  Seven Things You Should Know About Divine Healing
  El Shaddai
  Zoe: The God-Kind of Life
  A Commonsense Guide to Fasting
  Must Christians Suffer?
  The Woman Question
  The Believer's Authority
  Ministering to Your Family
  What To Do When Faith Seems Weak and Victory Lost
  Growing Up, Spiritually
  Bodily Healing and the Atonement (Dr. T.J. McCrossan)
  Exceedingly Growing Faith
  Understanding the Anointing
  I Believe in Visions
  Understanding How To Fight the Good Fight of Faith
  Plans, Purposes, and Pursuits
  How You Can Be Led by the Spirit of God
  A Fresh Anointing
  Classic Sermons
  He Gave Gifts Unto Men:
    A Biblical Perspective of Apostles, Prophets, and Pastors
  The Art of Prayer

Following God's Plan For Your Life
The Triumphant Church: Dominion Over All the Powers of Darkness
Healing Scriptures
Mountain Moving Faith
Love: The Way to Victory
Biblical Keys to Financial Prosperity
The Price Is Not Greater Than God's Grace (Mrs. Oretha Hagin)

MINIBOOKS (A partial listing)

* The New Birth
* Why Tongues?
* In Him
* God's Medicine
* You Can Have What You Say
* Don't Blame God
* Words
  Plead Your Case
* How To Keep Your Healing
  The Bible Way To Receive the Holy Spirit
  I Went to Hell
  How To Walk in Love
  The Precious Blood of Jesus
* Love Never Fails
  How God Taught Me About Prosperity

BOOKS BY KENNETH HAGIN JR.

* Man's Impossibility — God's Possibility
  Because of Jesus
  How To Make the Dream God Gave You Come True
  Forget Not!
  God's Irresistible Word
  Healing: Forever Settled
  Don't Quit! Your Faith Will See You Through
  The Untapped Power in Praise
  Listen to Your Heart
  What Comes After Faith?
  Speak to Your Mountain!
  Come Out of the Valley!
  It's Your Move!
  God's Victory Plan

MINIBOOKS (A partial listing)

* Faith Worketh by Love
* Seven Hindrances to Healing
* The Past Tense of God's Word
  Faith Takes Back What the Devil's Stolen
    How To Be a Success in Life
  Get Acquainted With God
    Unforgiveness
  Ministering to the Brokenhearted

*These titles are also available in Spanish. Information about other foreign translations of several of the above titles (i.e., Finnish, French, German, Indonesian, Polish, Russian, etc.) may be obtained by writing to: Kenneth Hagin Ministries, P.O. Box 50126, Tulsa, Oklahoma 74150-0126.

Contents

1. How Faith Comes 1

2. Now Faith Is 13

3. The Heart of Man 27

4. What It Means To Believe with the Heart 43

5. How To Train the Human Spirit 59

6. How To Write Your Own Ticket with God 73

7. The God-Kind of Faith 95

Chapter 1
How Faith Comes

But without faith it is impossible to please him: for he that cometh to God must believe that he is, and that he is a rewarder of them that diligently seek him.

— Hebrews 11:6

Notice particularly the first part of that verse, *"But without faith it is impossible to please him ...."*
If God demands that we have faith when it is impossible for us to have faith, then we have a right to challenge His justice. But if He places within our hands the means whereby faith can be produced, then the responsibility rests with us as to whether or not we have faith.

God has told us that without faith it is impossible to please Him, but He has also told us how to obtain faith. He has told us how faith comes.

ROMANS 10:17
17 So then faith cometh by hearing, and hearing by the word of God.

If we don't have faith, it is not God's fault. To blame God for our lack of faith is nothing but ignorance. God has provided the way whereby everyone can have faith.

Faith for Salvation

Faith for salvation *"cometh by hearing, and hearing by the word of God."*
The Apostle Paul said that we are saved by faith. *"For by grace are ye saved through faith; and that not of*

1

yourselves: it is the gift of God" (Eph. 2:8).

But how do you get the faith to be saved? Let's read more from this passage in Romans.

> **ROMANS 10:8-10,13,14,17**
> 8   But what saith it? The word is nigh thee, even in thy mouth, and in thy heart: that is, the word of faith, which we preach;
> 9   That if thou shalt confess with thy mouth the Lord Jesus, and shalt believe in thine heart that God hath raised him from the dead, thou shalt be saved.
> 10 For with the heart man believeth unto righteousness; and with the mouth confession is made unto salvation.
> 13 For whosoever shall call upon the name of the Lord shall be saved.
> 14 How then shall they call on him in whom they have not believed? and how shall they believe in him of whom they have not heard? and how shall they hear without a preacher?
> 17 So then faith cometh by hearing, and hearing by the word of God.

We see here that faith for salvation comes by *hearing the Word* of God. Now relate that with Acts 11:13,14, *"And he shewed us how he* [Cornelius] *had seen an angel in his house, which stood and said unto him, Send men to Joppa, and call for Simon, whose surname is Peter; WHO SHALL TELL THEE WORDS, whereby thou and all thy house shall be saved."*

Cornelius was a good man, but he was not saved. Jesus said, *"Go ye into all the world, and preach the gospel to every creature"* (Mark 16:15). As Cornelius had not as yet heard this glorious Gospel, he was not saved.

God told Cornelius to send for Peter in order to learn the plan of salvation. The angel could not preach to Cornelius. (Angels cannot preach — God sent men to preach.) But the angel could tell Cornelius where to go to get somebody ".... *who shall tell thee words whereby thou and all thy house shall be saved.*"

Men are saved by hearing words. And that is because "...*faith cometh by hearing, and hearing by the word of God.*" You cannot believe without hearing the Word.

Faith for Healing

How does faith for healing come? In the same way. You can see this in the following passage:

> ACTS 14:7-10
> 7 And there they [Paul and Barnabas] preached the gospel.
> 8 And there sat a certain man at Lystra, impotent in his feet, being a cripple from his mother's womb, who never had walked:
> 9 The same heard Paul speak: who stedfastly beholding him, and perceiving that he had faith to be healed,
> 10 Said with a loud voice, Stand upright on thy feet. And he leaped and walked.

A casual reader of the Word might say, "It is wonderful how Paul healed that man!" But Paul did not heal the man. The man was not healed because Paul was an apostle, nor was he healed by Paul's faith. *The man himself had the faith.*

Paul did three things:

1. He preached the Gospel (verse 7).
2. He perceived that the man had faith to be healed (verse 9).
3. He told the man to stand up and walk (verse 10).

The man did three things:
1. He heard Paul preach (verse 9).
2. He had faith to be healed (verse 9).
3. He leaped and walked (verse 10).

This man was not healed by some power which Paul had. The man himself had faith to be healed. And how did he get the faith to be healed? He got it from what he *heard.* He *heard* Paul speak.

And what did Paul speak? He preached the Gospel (verse 7).

If Paul had preached what some have called the Gospel, the man would have never been healed. Paul preached what the Bible calls the Gospel!

As a young Baptist boy on the bed of sickness reading Grandma's "Methodist" Bible, the more I read the more I realized that I had never heard the full Gospel, but only part of it. The more I read the Word, the more I noticed that I didn't have to die. The more I read, the more I realized that I could be healed!

(I had been taught that God could heal if He wanted to, which was an even bigger insult than saying He couldn't heal — both are lies.)

As I read the Word, though, the devil was right there trying to bring to my remembrance all the doubt and unbelief I had ever heard. He reminded me that I had heard that healing had been done away with.

But do you know how I was able to overcome that obstacle? I could never remember having heard anyone say that *faith* had been done away with!

This crippled man at Lystra had *faith* to be healed. In Mark 5:34 Jesus said to the woman who had just been healed from the issue of blood, *"Daughter, thy FAITH hath made thee whole.* "

Faith has not been done away with! It comes by
hearing — and hearing by the Word of God!

Jesus did not say that it was *His power* which made
the woman whole; He said that *her faith* did it. When I
saw this, I knew that if *her* faith made her whole, then
my faith could make *me* whole. And, thank God, it did!
My faith made me whole. My paralysis disappeared and
my heart condition left. Since then I have been going at
a hop, skip, and a jump, preaching the truth.

How did this man at Lystra get faith to be healed?
From what he *heard.* And what he heard was the Word
of God, the Gospel.

Is there something about the Gospel that would cause
a life-long cripple to be healed? Decidedly yes!

Paul preached a Gospel of salvation and of healing,
stating, *"For I am not ashamed of the gospel of Christ:
for it is the power of God unto salvation to every one that
believeth; to the Jew first, and also to the Greek"*
(Rom. 1:16).

A footnote in the Scofield Bible referring to this verse
says, "The Greek and Hebrew words for salvation imply
the ideas of *deliverance, safety, preservation, healing,* and
soundness. "

Therefore, Paul was saying, "I am not ashamed of the
Gospel of Christ. It is the power of God unto *deliverance,
safety, preservation, healing,* and *soundness.*" Paul preached
the *full* Gospel, not just a part of it.

ACTS 8:5-8
5 Then Philip went down to the city of Samaria, and
preached Christ unto them.

> 6   And the people with one accord gave heed unto those
> things which Philip spake, hearing and seeing the miracles
> which he did.
> 7   For unclean spirits, crying with loud voice, came out
> of many that were possessed with them: and many taken
> with palsies, and that were lame, were healed.
> 8   And there was great joy in that city.

These great miracles came about as a result of *preaching Christ* (verse 5). The New Testament knows no Christ without Christ the Healer. Physical healing — divine healing — is part of the Gospel. If there is no Gospel of healing today, neither is there a Gospel of salvation.

P. C. Nelson, who was for many years a noted Baptist minister, said, "Healing is part and parcel of the Gospel."

While pastoring a church in Detroit, Michigan, in 1921, Dr. Nelson was struck by an automobile. His left knee was severely injured. Blood poisoning developed, affecting his entire leg and threatening his life. His doctor warned that the leg might have to be amputated.

Even if he survived the blood poisoning and the leg didn't have to be amputated, the doctor said that leg would be stiff the rest of his life.

As Dr. Nelson lay immobile and in great pain, the Lord led him to read the entire Epistle of James. He realized he lacked faith for healing, but the story of Aeneas' healing in Acts 9:32-34 inspired faith in his heart.

The threat of a major operation prompted Dr. Nelson to renew his consecration and promise "to tell the world" if the Lord would heal him.

Then, desiring to obey James 5:14,15, he arranged for four Spirit-filled friends who had been healed themselves to come to his home, anoint him with oil, and pray. As they prayed, he seemed to hear the words of Acts 9:34, "Jesus Christ healeth thee. Arise!"

While his friends waited downstairs, Dr. Nelson dressed with the help of his son. Suddenly he realized his knee was completely free from pain. He joyously ran up and down stairs several times, rejoicing in the Lord. He was totally healed and never suffered stiffness in that knee. *"Faith cometh by hearing, and hearing by the word of God."*

Many years ago, a fine denominational minister had an outstanding evangelistic ministry. Various denominational churches would combine their efforts and sponsor him in large city-wide meetings. He became sick, however, and by his own testimony within two years all his money was gone.

A $10,000 bank account, which was quite a bit at that time, was gone. In order to pay medical bills he had to sell his home, his car, and most of his books. He had been everywhere, including the Mayo Clinic, seeking medical help. However, he was none the better, but rather grew worse. Finally he was forced to stay in a county hospital in California. The doctors there said he would die.

He called a brother who lived in California and asked him to borrow some money for a train ticket to send him home to Texas to die. Their 83-year-old mother lived in Collin County, Texas (where I lived), and he wanted to see her before he died.

His brother borrowed the money and sent the ailing minister, then in his 50's, back to the old home place and their aged mother. A 19-year-old boy who lived on the place and did the chores became the sick man's nurse. This required turning him, dressing him, and completely caring for him.

One day the boy said to him, "Doctor, why don't you let the Lord heal you? The Bible says that if there is any sick among you, let them call for the elders of the church and let them pray for you."

This minister had studied the Bible — he had been through seminary — but he did not know that was in the Bible. He instructed the boy to get his Bible out of the trunk and find that place.

But the boy told him that he had never learned to read. The minister asked him then how he knew that it was in the Bible. His preacher told him that it was, the boy declared. And so the minister looked it up and there it was!

The boy told him that they were having a meeting under a brush arbor. There was to be a healing service that night, and the boy told the older man that if he wanted to go he would get someone to take him. The minister decided to attend, so they brought an old Model T Ford and made a bed in the back of it for him. They drove the car up as close as possible, and after the service the preacher came out, anointed him with oil, and prayed over him.

It was midnight before they got home. But when they arrived, the minister asked his mother to let the boy fire up the wood stove so that she could fry some ham and eggs. (He hadn't had anything except baby food and soft foods in more than two years.)

He told his mother that he was healed. He told her that the preacher had anointed him with oil and prayed for him.

The mother said later that she thought he had lost his mind. He had asked for some old-fashioned country biscuits, too, and she reasoned that since he was going to die anyway, if he ate the biscuits he would at least die happy. So she did what he wanted. She fixed the ham, the eggs, and the biscuits — and he ate what she prepared and didn't get sick. He was healed!

He began to write articles for publication in various magazines and calls began to come in for revivals. A city-wide meeting was arranged for Kansas City.

The boy told him that before he went to that meeting he must be filled with the Holy Spirit. He said that he was ready to believe anything that boy told him, so he asked the boy what he should do. The boy told him how.

They went to an old brush arbor meeting, and when they gave the invitation, the minister went to the altar in the sawdust, and there he received the Holy Spirit and spoke with other tongues.

This minister has long since gone on to Glory, but his writings have been a blessing to many. Now how did this man get faith for healing? He got it by *hearing*.

I referred earlier to the woman who had an issue of blood for 12 years. The Word of God tells us about her in the fifth chapter of Mark. We are told that she had spent all of her living and had gone to many physicians, but was none better.

The 27th and 28th verses say about her, *"When she had HEARD of Jesus, came in the press behind, and touched his garment. For she said, If I may touch but his clothes, I shall be whole."* And in the 34th verse we read, *"And he said unto her, Daughter, thy faith hath made thee whole; go in peace, and be whole of thy plague."*

Where did this woman get faith to receive healing? *"When she had heard . . . ."* (v. 27).

After preaching several weeks in a Full Gospel church in Dallas during the early '50s, I stayed on three months while the pastor took a leave of absence. In addition to preaching at the regular church services, we also had a daily radio program.

One weekend we had some special missionary services. On Friday night, after the service had been dismissed, one of the ushers told me that a man and a woman from Fort Worth wanted to see me. The wife was sick and wanted healing.

Her husband related that as he drove to work one morning, he had heard our radio program. He had heard me make the statement that healing was for everybody, and he had gone home that night and told his wife about it. All that week they had tuned in to the radio broadcast.

This woman had had two serious major operations and was facing the third. "We have been praying," the husband said, "that if it is God's will for her to be healed, He will give us the faith to believe that she will be healed." And they had come for me to pray for her.

I began by telling them it is unscriptural to pray, "If it be Thy will" concerning anything which God's Word has already promised us. When you put an "if" in your prayer, you are praying in doubt.

Some people think they are being humble, when really they are being ignorant. You will get no answer if you put "if's" in your prayers when God's Word has already made His will plain.

It is only when you are praying a prayer of consecration that you put an "if" in the prayer. This is because in a prayer of consecration you are not certain what the Lord's will is.

"If" is the badge of doubt, and it should not be in your prayers when you are trying to change a situation.

I asked the husband, "If the New Testament said that Jesus took your wife's infirmities and bare her sicknesses, wouldn't it be His will for her to have her healing?"

He acknowledged that it would. So we turned in the Word to Matthew 8:17, which says, *"That it might be fulfilled which was spoken by Esaias the prophet, saying, Himself took our infirmities, and bare our sicknesses."*

"It *is* God's will for her to be healed!" he exclaimed. Then his wife said that she saw it, too.

We then turned to First Peter 2:24 and read, *"Who his own self bare our sins in his own body on the tree, that we, being dead to sins, should live unto righteousness: BY WHOSE STRIPES YE WERE HEALED"* (1 Peter 2:24).

And in Isaiah 53:4,5 we read together, *"Surely he hath borne our griefs, and carried our sorrows: yet we did esteem him stricken, smitten of God, and afflicted. But he was wounded for our transgressions, he was bruised for our iniquities: the chastisement of our peace was upon him; and WITH HIS STRIPES WE ARE HEALED."* The margin of the *King James Version* reads, "Surely he hath borne our sicknesses and carried our diseases."

So the couple said, "All we need now is faith. We know it is His will."

I asked them if they were saved, and they replied that they were. I asked them to describe how they had gotten saved. They stated that they had gone down to the front of the church when an invitation was given and had knelt and prayed a sinner's prayer.

"When you went down to the front," I asked, "did you ask the Lord to give you faith to be saved?" Their answer was no.

The husband said that the preacher had preached that

they could be saved. He had read the Word to the people. They had heard the Word and faith came for salvation.

I told them that they had faith for healing just as they had had faith for salvation. They had heard the Word.

"We're going to have to throw our first prayer away because it wasn't any good," the husband declared. I agreed with him. As soon as light comes, faith is there!

His wife agreed, saying, "I see that all I have to do now is to accept Him as my Healer."

I laid my hand on her head and prayed. Then I asked her if she were healed.

She confessed, "I surely am, and I know I am because God's Word says that I am."

During the following Sunday night service, the vestibule doors swung open and there stood her husband. After asking if he could say a word, he began to tell what had happened.

He said that when they arrived home that Friday night, his wife pulled off her brace, threw it into the closet and said, "Thank God, I am healed!" The next day, Saturday, when he came home he found his wife stooped over the sink, washing her hair — something she had been unable to do.

This Sunday night he brought his mother, who was in a wheelchair with paralysis, to be prayed for. After prayer she stood up and walked out!

When hands were laid on the young couple, they received the baptism in the Holy Spirit and began to speak in tongues. Years later I talked with them and she was still healed.

How did she get faith? From hearing the Word!

Chapter 2
Now Faith Is

Now faith is the substance of things hoped for, the evidence of things not seen.
— Hebrews 11:1

In Hebrews 11:1 God tells us what Bible faith is. Moffatt's translation of this verse reads, "Now faith means that we are confident of what we hope for, convinced of what we do not see." Another translation says, "Faith is giving substance to things hoped for." Still another translation reads, "Faith is the warranty deed, the thing for which we have finally hoped is at last ours."

There are a number of kinds of faith. Everyone, saved or unsaved, has a natural, human faith. But here God is talking about a scriptural faith. He is talking about a Bible faith. He is talking about believing with your heart. And there is a vast difference between believing with your heart and just believing what your physical senses tell you!

Faith is grasping the unrealities of hope and bringing them into the realm of reality.

For example, you hope for finances to meet the obligations that you have to pay. Faith gives the assurance that you will have the money when you need it. "Faith is the evidence of things not seen." You hope for physical strength to do the work that you must do. Faith says, *"The Lord is the strength of my life; of whom shall I be afraid"* (Ps. 27:1). Faith will say about itself everything that the Word says, *for faith in God is simply faith in His Word.*

In being raised from the bed of sickness many years ago, I learned what faith is. After getting healed, I needed work, and since it was during the Depression, work was

13

not easy to find. However, I was able to get a job in a nursery helping to pull up peach trees. With another boy on the other side of the tree, we would pull up two-year-old trees to fill orders that had come in. I want you to know that was work — especially for someone who had been bedfast for 16 months and at this time had been up only a few months.

Each morning before sunup we would meet, and every day some of the boys would say, "Well, I didn't think you'd make it today. You know, two or three quit yesterday."

Now I didn't believe in going around trying to push something off on someone, but I did believe in witnessing for God. And when they would say these things, it would give me the opportunity to witness.

"If it weren't for the Lord I wouldn't be here," I would answer, "for you see, His strength is my strength. The Bible says, *'The Lord is the strength of my life.'* My life consists of the physical as well as the spiritual, and the Lord is the strength of my life."

It would make some of the boys angry when I would say that. But I would smile and say, "Praise the Lord, I'll be here tomorrow and every other day, because the Lord is my strength."

Now, if I had gone by my feelings I would never have gotten out of bed! I was never so weak in my life. I felt as if I couldn't do it. But I stayed with it. I acted upon the Word because I knew what faith was.

I would say to the Father, to Jesus, to the Holy Spirit, to the devil, to myself, and to the other boys if they asked me, "The Lord is my strength." But I never actually got any help *until* I started to work.

Many people want to get something and then believe
they've got it. But you have to *believe* you have something
and then you *receive* it.

When we began to work each morning I wouldn't have
any strength, but when we started on the first tree (or
sometimes the second) I would feel something hit me in
the top of my head. It would go through my body, out the
ends of my fingers, and out the ends of my toes. Then I
would work all day long like a Trojan.

One 250-pound fellow said, "I'll tell you, when this old
250 pounds is gone, there won't be a man left in the field."
And I said, "Why, Alton, God weighs more than 250
pounds. When you fall out and quit, I'll still be here." That
riled him, but at 3 o'clock that afternoon he fell out and
I was the only man left. In the natural I was the weakest
and the skinniest, but I was the only man left of the
original crew. I had proved God's Word.

You may say that you know God's Word is good, but
you never will really know until you have *acted on it* and
have reaped the results.

And this is what I am trying to tell you that faith is.
Faith is giving substance to the things hoped for. I acted
on God's Word; I went to work. I hoped for the physical
strength to do the work, but it was my faith that gave
substance to what I had hoped for. Faith says, "God is
the strength of my life." As I acted on God's Word, faith
gave substance to that for which I had hoped.

A lot of people just hope — and stop there. And that
won't work. *Faith* is the *substance* of things hoped for.
If you say, "Well, I *hope* God heard my prayer," and that's
all you do, He didn't, and there won't be any answer. But
your faith can and will give substance to the answer to

that prayer.

Remember this: Hope says, "I will have it *sometime.*" Faith says, "I have it *now.*"   ·

John Wesley said, "The devil has given to the Church a substitute for faith which looks and sounds so much like faith some people can't tell the difference." He called it "mental assent."

Many people see what God's Word says and acknowledge that it is true — but it is only with their minds that they are agreeing. And that will not get the job done. It is *heart* faith that receives from God. Notice what the Bible says, *"For with the* heart *man believeth . . . ."* (Rom. 10:10).

Jesus said in Mark 11:23, ". . .*whosoever shall say unto this mountain, Be thou removed, and be thou cast into the sea; and shall not doubt in his heart* [this doesn't say a word about the head], *but shall believe* [that is, with the heart] *that those things which he saith shall come to pass; he shall have whatsoever he saith."*

You may ask, "How can I tell whether I have heart faith or whether I am just agreeing with my head?" If it is merely mental agreement or mental assent it says, "I know God's Word is true. I know God promises me healing or the Holy Spirit, but for some reason I can't get it. And I can't understand it."

Real faith in God's Word says, "If God's Word says it is so, then it is so. It is mine. I have it *now."* Real faith also says, "I have it when I can't see it."

Our text declares that faith is *"the evidence of things not seen."* One who has not prayed in real heart faith might say, "I don't see the thing about which I have been praying, so it hasn't come to pass." If the thing had come to pass — if you had it — you wouldn't have to believe it; you would *know* it.

You must take the step of *believing* to come to the place of *knowing*. Many want to know it first and then believe it. That is, they want to know it from the standpoint of its having come to pass. But we know it from the standpoint that God's Word says it is so — then it materializes.

Notice what Jesus says in Mark 11:24, *"What things soever ye desire, when ye pray, BELIEVE that ye receive them, and ye shall HAVE them."* Now notice that the having comes *after* the believing. Most people want to turn that around. In common, everyday terms Jesus said, "You have to believe you've got it before you get it."

I never have been able to receive healing for my body without believing first that I had it, even while every symptom in my body was crying out, "You don't have healing." I would simply say to my flesh, "The Bible says, *'let God be true, but every man a liar . . . .'* So if you say I am not healed, you are a liar. God's Word says that I am healed." When I act like that, results are forthcoming one hundred times out of one hundred.

Conversely, if a person sits around and groans, sighs, gripes, and complains, waiting for something to happen — waiting until he can detect that every symptom is gone and all the flesh corresponds with his faith before he starts believing God — he is out of order, and he will never get very far.

Thomas said, "I will not believe until I can see Him and put my finger in the print in His hands, and thrust my hand into the wound in His side." Then when Jesus appeared, Thomas said, *"My Lord and my God"* (John 20:28).

Jesus said to Thomas, "Because you have seen, you have believed." In other words, Thomas wasn't believing in the same way you and I believe in Jesus' resurrection. He believed because he saw Him with his physical eye. We believe it because the Word of God says it is so.

Some people miss it without realizing it. They say, "Well, I believe in divine healing because I saw So-and-so healed." That's not the reason I believe in divine healing. I believe it because the Word of God says it.

Likewise, I don't believe in speaking in tongues because some people believe in it and speak with tongues. I believe what the Bible says; not what I see and hear. *My faith is not in what I see and hear.* My faith is in what God says. When we get our faith to that point, we are right and in order, and that brings results.

Thomas said, in effect, "I will not believe until I see." And Jesus said, "Thomas, thou hast believed because thou hast seen; blessed are they who have not seen, yet do believe." Those are the ones who are blessed!

Compare now Thomas' faith with the faith of Abraham:

ROMANS 4:17-21
17 (As it is written, I have made thee [Abraham] a father of many nations,) before him whom he believed, even God, who quickeneth the dead, and calleth those things which be not as though they were.
18 Who against hope believed in hope, that he might become the father of many nations, according to that which was spoken, So shall thy seed be.
19 And being not weak in faith, he considered not his own body now dead, when he was about an hundred years old, neither yet the deadness of Sarah's womb:
20 He staggered not at the promise of God through unbelief; but was strong in faith, giving glory to God;

21 And being fully persuaded that, what he had promised, he was able also to perform.

Notice the difference between Thomas' faith and Abraham's faith. Thomas had only a natural, human faith which said, "I'm not going to believe unless I can see and feel." Abraham, however, believed God's Word, considering not his own body. If he didn't consider his own body, he didn't consider physical sight or physical feelings. Then what did he consider? *The Word of God!*

A number of years ago after I was healed of heart trouble, I was struggling along some of the same lines many people do. Alarming heart symptoms seemed to return to me. In the night I would have some terrible struggles, and although I had been praying and standing on the promises, I couldn't get off to sleep.

I said, "Lord, I have to have some relief." And then He told me, "Consider not thine own body." So I just relaxed and said, "Thank You," and took my mind off my body and drifted off to sleep.

I awoke again and had some of the same symptoms. I said, "Lord, if I'm not considering my own body, what am I supposed to consider?" He said, "Consider Him who is the Author and Finisher of your faith, your High Priest." He told me what not to consider and then what to consider.

Immediately, I got my mind on Him, and I began to consider what He had done for us. I considered that *"Himself took our infirmities, and bare our sicknesses"* (Matt. 8:17). As I considered not my own body, but got my mind and attention on Him, I drifted off to sleep and every symptom left.

Too often we focus our attention on the wrong thing. We consider the body and the symptoms when it comes to healing. That's what we think about and look at, and the more we look at it, the worse we get. Some will even say, "Well, God hasn't heard my prayer yet. I'm getting worse. I guess I'll wind up being operated on." And they will!

In one church where I held meetings, there was a woman who testified every time she could. And at the end of every testimony she would say, "You all pray for me. I believe I've got cancer." Finally, the pastor got tired of it and when she got through he stood and said, "That's right, Sister. Keep believing it and you will get it, for Jesus said, 'According to your faith be it unto you.' "

Some people say, "Brother Hagin, pray for me. I believe I am taking a cold." It wouldn't do any good for me to pray, because if they *believe* they are taking it, they *will* take it. "According to your faith be it unto you." If you keep believing for it, you will get it. Do not consider and see the wrong thing.

Some people only get a part of what I am saying. They think I am teaching like Christian Science and saying to deny all symptoms and just go on as if they weren't even there. But there is as much difference in what I am teaching and what Christian Science teaches as there is between daylight and dark. As one doctor said, "This is not Christian Science; this is Christian sense."

We do not deny these things, because they are real. Certainly pain is real. Sin is real. And the devil is real. But notice what God's Word said, "Abraham considered not his own body." So don't consider your body, but do consider Jesus, our High Priest, the Author and Finisher of our faith.

Focus your attention on what He *has* done for you and on what He *is* doing for you because He is our High Priest. He is doing something for you right now. He is up there by the throne of God making intercession for you.

HEBREWS 4:14
14 Seeing then that we have a great high priest, that is passed into the heavens, Jesus the Son of God, let us hold fast our profession [confession].

I want you to notice this: *"Seeing then that we have a great high priest. . . ."* Or, if you like, "This is the reason we must hold fast to our confession because we have such a great high priest."

In looking up the Greek word for "confession," I found out that it says, "Let us hold fast to saying the same things."

Jesus is up there representing us at the throne of God, and He is saying, "I took their place. I died for them as their Substitute." He didn't die for Himself. He didn't need to redeem Himself — He wasn't lost. He died for us. He became *my* Substitute. He took my sins. He bore my sickness. He carried my diseases. He died for me. He arose from the dead for me. He ascended on high for me, and He is up there right now saying, "I did that for him."

And we are to hold fast to *saying the same thing* down here. That is what puts the devil on the run. Focus your attention on the right things rather than on yourself.

PROVERBS 4:20-22
20 My son, attend to my words; incline thine ear unto my sayings.

21 Let them [my words] not depart from thine eyes; keep
them in the midst of thine heart.
22 For they [my words] are life unto those that find them,
and health to all their flesh.

Many people fail *because they see themselves fail.* A
turning point came in my life when I first saw this Scripture. Until that time I had always seen myself dead. I could
picture every detail about it. But after I read this Scripture, I could see myself well. I began to see myself alive.
And I began to see myself doing things I had never done
because of my heart condition.

I knew God had called me to preach, and I could see
myself preaching. I began to get ready for it. I asked for
a tablet and pencil and I got my Bible and began to prepare
sermons. They weren't preachable — only one was ever
preached — but I was getting ready. *Many people fail
because they get ready to fail.*

Notice what He says: *"Let them* [my words] *not depart
from thine eyes."* Now think for a moment. Don't you
know that if God's Word says in Matthew 8:17 that Jesus
took your infirmities, and bare your diseases, and if you
do not let that Word depart from before your eyes, you
are bound to see yourself without sickness and without
disease?

You will see yourself well! If you do not see yourself
without sickness and disease and if you do not see yourself
well, then that Word has departed from before your eyes.
And even though He *wants* to make His Word good in
your life, He *cannot,* because you are not acting on His
Word!

It is difficult for me to follow the reasoning of some
people that God is going to do something for them without

their doing what the Word says. He is not! God cannot!
Even though He wants to, He cannot. You see, if He did,
He would be violating His Word and making Himself to
be a liar, and the Bible says God cannot lie.

Right here in Proverbs God tells us that His Word is
medicine to us. In the 22nd verse He says, *"For they* [my
words] *are life unto those that find them, and health to
all their flesh."*

The Hebrew word translated "health" is also the word
for "medicine." In other words, "My Words are *medicine*
to all their flesh." But in order for medicine to be effec-
tive, it must be taken according to directions. And the first
two verses (verses 20 and 21) give you the directions for
taking the medicine!

Does God have any medicine? Yes, thank God, He does.
His Words are life unto those who find them and medicine
to all their flesh. However, that medicine must be taken
according to directions, and one of the directions is, *"Let
them* [my words] *not depart from thine eyes."* Keep looking at what the Word says!

If God's Word says He heard and answered your prayer,
and if that Word does not depart from before your eyes,
then you are going to see yourself with what you prayed for!

Many are defeated in their prayer lives because they
do not *see themselves with the answer.* They just see
everything getting worse. They look at the wrong things,
so they walk in unbelief and destroy the effects of their
praying.

Get your mind on the answer. Constantly affirm, even
in the face of contradictory evidence, that God has heard
your prayer because the Word says so. It is when you do
not let His Words depart from before your eyes that you
will get results.

This all agrees with what Jesus says in Mark 11:24, *"...What things soever ye desire, when ye pray, believe that ye receive them, and ye shall have them."* You must believe it before you receive it.

Some say, "I'm not going to believe anything I can't see," when even in the physical, or the natural, we believe many things we can't see.

The entire world became concerned about something they couldn't see when bombs were being exploded which released radioactive material into the atmosphere. We can't see it and we can't feel it — but it is a destructive power. Scientists believe in many things they can't see. And then some think it is preposterous for God to call upon us to believe in the unseen!

Just as people became alarmed about the unseen radioactivity in this world and believed it even though they could not see it or feel it, I believe what the Word of God says about the Holy Spirit — the unseen power of God — whether or not I feel it or see it.

Some of the greatest healings which have taken place in our meetings were when I didn't *feel* a thing. Some of the most marvelous things have happened when the service seemed dead. Feeling has nothing to do with it. God is present. His power is present. *I do not base my faith on what I feel.* I base it on what God said. And He said, *"I will never leave thee, nor forsake thee."*

Remember that He said in Hebrews 13:5,6, *"...for he hath said, I will never leave thee, nor forsake thee. So that we may boldly say, The Lord is my helper, and I will not fear what man shall do unto me."*

Is that what you are saying? Are you boldly saying, *"The Lord is my helper"*? It is what you should be saying!

But some people are saying, "Well, the Lord's forsaken me; pray for me. I just don't feel like I once did." Your feelings have nothing whatsoever to do with this. The Lord has said He would never forsake you!

And some say, "Well, I don't know whether I can make it or not. I hope I can. You all pray for me that I'll hold out faithful to the end." That is not what He told us to boldly say!

Many are boldly saying, "I'm whipped. I'm defeated. The devil's got me bound." But nowhere in the Bible are we told to boldly say that!

He said, "I will never leave you, nor forsake you, so that you may boldly say, 'The Lord is my helper.' " Now quit saying the wrong thing and start saying the right thing.

Say, "The Lord is my helper." Is He?

Say, "The Lord is my healer." Is He?

Say, "He took my infirmities and bare my sicknesses." Didn't He?

Keep talking about the right thing. Believe the right thing.

It is simply wrong thinking, wrong believing, and wrong talking which defeats people. You see, the devil can't defeat you. Jesus has already defeated the devil for you. Satan doesn't defeat you; you defeat yourself! (Or, if Satan does, it is because you permit him to do so. It is a consent of ignorance.)

God has given us His Word to get our thinking straightened out so that our believing will be right. If our thinking is right and our believing is right, then our talking will be right.

The Lord is my helper. The Lord is my strength. Real

faith in the Word says, "If God says it is so — then it is so. If He says, 'By His stripes ye were healed' — then I am healed. If He says, 'God shall supply my every need' — then He does. If God says, 'He is the strength of my life' — then He is."

In other words, *real faith in God simply says about one's self what the Word says.*

Thank God, I have what the Word says I have! I am what the Word says I am! If He says I am strong — I am! If He says I am healed — I am! If He says He cares for me — He does! So I simply, quietly, rest on the Word. For the Word says, *"For we which have believed do enter into rest...."* (Heb. 4:3). I believe and therefore I quietly rest on the Word regardless of evidence that would satisfy the physical or the natural.

Real faith is built on the Word. Meditate on the Word. Dig deeply into it. Feed upon it. Then the Word will become part of you, just as natural food becomes a part of your physical body when you eat.

What natural food is to the physical man, the Word of God is to the spiritual man. The Word will build into you — the real you, the inward man — confidence and assurance. Faith comes by hearing, and hearing by the Word of God.

Chapter 3
The Heart of Man

For with the heart man believeth unto righteousness; and with the mouth confession is made unto salvation.

— Romans 10:10

For verily I say unto you, That whosoever shall say unto this mountain, Be thou removed, and be thou cast into the sea; and shall not doubt in his heart, but shall believe that those things which he saith shall come to pass; he shall have whatsoever he saith.

— Mark 11:23

Both of the preceding verses speak of believing with the heart. Notice the expressions, *"For with the heart man believeth"* and *"shall not doubt in his heart, but shall believe."* For years I eagerly searched for a satisfactory explanation of what it means to believe "with the heart."

You must understand, of course, that the word "heart" as used in these Scriptures does not refer to the physical organ which pumps blood through the body and keeps us alive.

The word "heart" here cannot refer to that human physical organ, for if it did, these verses would indicate that you could believe with your *body.* And you could no more believe God with your physical heart than you could believe Him with your physical hand or finger.

The word "heart" is used here to convey a thought. Consider how we use "heart" today. When we talk about the heart of a tree, what do we mean? We mean the center,

27

the very core. When we talk about the heart of a subject, what do we mean? We mean the most important part of that subject, the center of it, the main part around which the rest revolves. And when God speaks of the human heart, He is speaking about the main part of man; the very center of man's being — the spirit.

Man is a Spirit

1 THESSALONIANS 5:23
23 And the very God of peace sanctify you wholly; and I pray God your whole spirit and soul and body be preserved blameless unto the coming of our Lord Jesus Christ.

The terms "spirit of man" and "heart of man" are used interchangeably throughout the Bible. We know that man is a spirit because he is made in the image and likeness of God, and Jesus said, *"God is a Spirit"* (John 4:24). It is not in our physical bodies that we are like God, for the Bible says that God is not a man.

Paul said in his letter to the Romans, *"For he is not a Jew, which is one outwardly; neither is that circumcision, which is outward in the flesh: But he is a Jew, which is one inwardly; and circumcision is that OF THE HEART, IN THE SPIRIT, and not in the letter; whose praise is not of men, but of God"* (Rom. 2:28,29). According to this verse, the heart is the spirit.

Speaking to Nicodemus, Jesus said, *"Ye must be born again"* (John 3:7).

Nicodemus, being human, or natural, could think only in the natural, and therefore he asked, *"How can a man be born when he is old? can he enter the second time into his mother's womb, and be born?"* (v. 4).

Jesus replied, *"That which is born of the flesh is flesh;
and that which is born of the Spirit is spirit"* (v. 6). *The
New Birth is a rebirth of the human spirit.*

Jesus told the woman at the well in Samaria, *"God is
a Spirit: and they that worship him must worship him in
spirit and in truth"* (John 4:24). We cannot contact God
with our *body* or with our *mind.* We can contact God only
with our *spirit.*

The spirit is not the mind. First Corinthians 14:14 says,
*"For if I pray in an unknown tongue, my spirit prayeth,
but my understanding* [mind] *is unfruitful."*

Some people mistakenly think that the mind is the
spirit. However, as this verse indicates, we know that when
we speak in tongues, this does not come from our mind,
or out of our own human thinking, but from our spirit, from
our innermost being, from the Holy Spirit within our spirit.

Paul went on to say, *"What is it then? I will pray with
the spirit, and I will pray with the understanding also...."*
(v. 15).

The following beautiful passage speaks of *"the spirits
of just men made perfect."*

HEBREWS 12:18-24
18 For ye are not come unto the mount that might be
touched, and that burned with fire, nor unto blackness, and
darkness, and tempest,
19 And the sound of a trumpet, and the voice of words;
which voice they that heard intreated that the word should
not be spoken to them any more:
20 (For they could not endure that which was commanded,
And if so much as a beast touch the mountain, it shall be
stoned, or thrust through with a dart:
21 And so terrible was the sight, that Moses said, I exceedingly fear and quake:)

22 But ye are come unto mount Sion, and unto the city of
the living God, the heavenly Jerusalem, and to an innumer-
able company of angels,
23 To the general assembly and church of the first born,
which are written in heaven, and to God the Judge of all,
and to the spirits of just men made perfect,
24 And to Jesus the mediator of the new covenant, and
to the blood of sprinkling . . . .

As we look into God's Word I want you to become conscious of this fact: *You are a spirit; you have a soul; and
you live in a body.*

The Inward Man

2 CORINTHIANS 4:16
16 For which cause we faint not; but though our outward
man perish, yet the inward man is renewed day by day.

There is an inward man and an outward man. The outward man is the body. The inward man is the spirit — and
the spirit has a soul.

1 CORINTHIANS 9:27
27 But I keep under my body, and bring it into subjection:
lest that by any means, when I have preached to others,
I myself should be a castaway.

Now notice something here. If the body were the real
man, Paul would have said, "I keep myself under; I bring
myself into subjection." But Paul refers to his body as
"it." "I" is the man on the inside, the inward man who
has been reborn. And Paul said in effect, "*I* do something
with *my body. I* bring *it* into subjection." You see, the

outward man which we look at is not the real man, but only the house the real man lives in.

We can now more easily understand Paul's writings to the saints at Rome:

> **ROMANS 12:1,2**
> 1 I beseech you therefore, brethren, by the mercies of God, that ye present your bodies a living sacrifice, holy, acceptable unto God, which is your reasonable service.
> 2 And be not conformed to this world: but be ye transformed by the renewing of your mind, that ye may prove what is that good, and acceptable, and perfect, will of God.

I had preached for more than 20 years before I saw something in this Scripture which astounded me. Paul is not writing this to unbelievers, but to Christians. The letter was addressed, *"To all that be in Rome, beloved of God, called to be saints . . . ."* (Rom. 1:7). He is writing to men and women who have been born again and filled with the Holy Spirit, yet he says to them, "You need to do something with your bodies and your minds."

It came as a shock to me when I saw that here were people who were saved and filled with the Holy Spirit, yet their bodies and minds had not been affected.

The New Birth is not a rebirth of the human body, but a rebirth of the human spirit. And the infilling of the Holy Spirit is not a physical experience, but a spiritual experience.

According to these verses of Scripture, *we* have to do something with our bodies. *We* have to present them to God a living sacrifice. And *we* have to do something with our minds. *We* have to get them renewed with the Word.

This is something that we do, not something God does.
God gives eternal life. He offers us His Spirit. But God
doesn't do anything with our bodies. If anything is done
with your body, you will have to do it.
The Word says for *you* to present your body unto God.
Nobody else can do it for you. The Word says that *you*
are to be "transformed by the renewing of your mind."
And your mind is renewed through the Word of God.

Man is a spirit. He is in the same class with God —
made in the image and likeness of God. Some would have
you believe that man is just an animal. If that were true,
it would be no more wrong to kill a man and eat him than
it would be to kill a cow and eat it.

Man has a physical body in which he now lives, but
he is not an animal. He is much more than just mind and
body. He is spirit, soul, and body. He is a spirit; he has
a soul; he lives in a body.

It is the fact that man is a spirit that makes him different from animals. Some false cults bring out that in
Genesis, in the Hebrew language, the Word of God speaks
of the souls of animals. They say that since animals have
souls as we do, then when we die we are dead as a dog is
dead. And they interpret all Scripture from the natural
view.

And it is true that animals have souls — but they are
not spirits! In Christendom we have not defined these
terms as we should have. There is nothing in animals which
is like God.

God took something of Himself and put it into man.
He made the body of man out of the dust of the earth; but
He breathed into man's nostrils the breath of life.

The word translated "breath" in the passage concerning

man's creation, is the Hebrew word *ruach*. *Ruach* means "breath" or "spirit," and it is translated "Holy Spirit" many times in the Old Testament. God is *spirit*, so He took something of Himself, which is *spirit*, and put it into man. When He did, man became a living soul. He wasn't alive until then. But he became a living soul — he became conscious of himself.

Animals have souls, for the soul possesses intellectual and emotional qualities, and animals have these. However, in animals, it is all physical, and when the physical is dead, all is gone.

Man's soul — his intellectual and emotional qualities — is not based upon the physical, but upon the spirit. And when the body is dead, the spirit with its soul still exists.

LUKE 16:19-31

19 There was a certain rich man, which was clothed in purple and fine linen, and fared sumptuously every day:

20 And there was a certain beggar named Lazarus, which was laid at his gate, full of sores,

21 And desiring to be fed with the crumbs which fell from the rich man's table: moreover the dogs came and licked his sores.

22 And it came to pass, that the beggar died, and was carried by the angels into Abraham's bosom: the rich man also died, and was buried;

23 And in hell he lift up his eyes, being in torments, and seeth Abraham afar off, and Lazarus in his bosom.

24 And he cried and said, Father Abraham, have mercy on me, and send Lazarus, that he may dip the tip of his finger in water, and cool my tongue; for I am tormented in this flame.

25 But Abraham said, Son, remember that thou in thy lifetime receivedst thy good things, and likewise Lazarus evil things: but now he is comforted, and thou art tormented.

26 And beside all this, between us and you there is a great

gulf fixed: so that they which would pass from hence to you cannot; neither can they pass to us, that would come from thence.
27 Then he said, I pray thee therefore, father, that thou wouldest send him to my father's house:
28 For I have five brethren; that he may testify unto them, lest they also come into this place of torment.
29 Abraham saith unto him, They have Moses and the prophets; let them hear them.
30 And he said, Nay, father Abraham: but if one went unto them from the dead, they will repent.
31 And he said unto him, If they hear not Moses and the prophets, neither will they be persuaded, though one rose from the dead.

In this passage, we have a very vivid illustration of man's three parts: spirit, soul, and body.

Notice that verse 22 says, *"the beggar died, and was carried by the angels into Abraham's bosom."* Who was carried away? The beggar — not his body — was carried away. His spirit is the real person. His body was put into the grave, but *he* was in Abraham's bosom.

The rich man also died. His body was put into the grave, but *"in hell HE lift up his eyes."* And, although Abraham's body had been in the grave for many years, the rich man saw *him.*

Also, the rich man recognized Lazarus. Therefore, *in the spirit realm, man's appearance is similar to his appearance in this life.* You can recognize him. You can know who he is.

When the rich man cried out to Abraham, Abraham said to him, "Son, remember . . . ." Man is a spirit and he has a soul. We see in this Scripture that his soul is still intact. He can still remember. He still has emotion. He is concerned about his five brothers.

I Went to Hell

I always have been interested in this realm because, as I have preached many times, I went to hell. It was on April 22, 1933, Saturday night at 7:30, in the south bedroom of 405 North College Street in the city of McKinney, Texas. Just as Grandpa's old clock on the mantelpiece struck 7:30, my heart stopped within my bosom and I felt the circulation cut off down at the end of my toes and all the way up to my heart.

Then I had the sensation of leaping out of my body. I knew I was out of my body, yet I was no less man than when I was in my body.

I began to descend. Down, down, down I went, as if I were going down into a pit or well. I looked up and I could see the lights of earth far above me. The farther down I went, the darker it became. Finally, darkness encompassed me; darkness darker than any night man has ever seen; darkness so dense it seemed that with a knife a piece could be cut out of it. And the farther down I went, the hotter it became. It was stifling.

My mind, my soul, was intact. I thought of life, and my entire past came up before me.

Still descending, I saw down before me fingers of light playing on the wall of darkness. I saw out in front of me a giant orange flame with a white crest. Then I came to the gate, the entrance, or the portals of hell itself.

A creature of some kind met me when I reached the bottom of the pit. Even though I knew he was by my side, I didn't look at him. My gaze was riveted on hell. During the descent, I had intended to put up a fight, if I could,

to keep from going in. At the entrance I paused momen-
tarily, although never coming to a complete stop.

When I did that, the creature by my side took me by
the arm. Now my physical body was still lying on the bed,
but there is a spiritual body. That spiritual body has arms,
and eyes, and ears — all the features the physical body
has. The rich man said, "I am tormented in the flame."
He *saw* Lazarus and recognized him. Actually I could not
tell any difference in myself, except that I could not contact the physical and I was not living in the physical realm.

Bible scholars agree that Paul was talking about his
own experience when he wrote, *"I knew a man in Christ
above fourteen years ago, (whether in the body, I cannot
tell; or whether out of the body, I cannot tell: God knoweth;)
such an one caught up to the third heaven"* (2 Cor. 12:2).
I know what Paul meant when he said that he didn't know
if he was in the body, or out of the body.

Just as that creature took me by the arm to escort me
in, a voice spoke. It was a male voice. I heard it as it boomed
and echoed. I could not understand what the voice said,
as it spoke in a tongue other than English. But when He
said whatever He said (from six to nine words), that whole
place shook and quivered like a leaf in the wind.

Then that creature took his hand off my arm and
something like a suction, an irresistible pull to my back,
without turning me around, pulled me away from the entrance of hell, back through the shadows of the pit, and
I came up head first to the porch outside that south
bedroom. Just for a second I knew that I was standing
on the porch. Then I went right through the wall. (Material
things have no effect on spiritual things.) I seemed to leap
inside my body. Back inside my body, I could contact the

physical again.

To my grandmother, who had held my head in her lap and bathed my face with a cool, damp cloth, I said, "Granny, I'm dying."

"Son, I thought you were gone."

As I felt myself slipping away again I said, "I'm going again and I won't be back this time."

The entire scene was repeated three times.

Shortly after this experience, as I began to pray, I was saved — born again.

And four months later, on August 16, 1933 at 1:30 in the afternoon, again I knew I was dying. My youngest brother was standing beside my bed and I told him to get Mother quickly.

Just as Momma came into the room, I had the same sensation I'd had before. But this time I was saved! As I leaped out of my body and left it, I began to ascend. This time I didn't go down; I went up.

Our old-fashioned house had high ceilings and when I got up to about where the roof of the house should have been, approximately 16 feet above the bed, my ascent stopped and I seemed to stand there. I was fully conscious and knew everything that was going on.

Looking back into the room, I saw my body lying on the bed and my mother stooped over it holding my hand in hers. (She told me later that I had held her hand in a death-like grip.) But I had left my body, and I could not speak to my mother to tell her good-by.

Then I heard a voice and I looked up. I saw no one, but I heard a male voice. I don't know whether it was Jesus, an angel, or who it was, but I know it was an emissary of heaven. This time the voice did not speak in a foreign tongue, but in English.

"Go back. Go back. Go back. You can't come yet. Your work on earth is not done."

When those words were spoken, I began to descend and I came back into my body.

And back inside my body I said, "Momma, I'm not going to die now." She thought that I wasn't going to die at that moment, but I meant that I was not going to die at all then. I meant that I was going to live my life out and do the work of God.

But I stayed in that bed almost 12 months to the day before I received my healing. For, even though it was the will of God for me to live, He couldn't make an exception of me. I had to receive my healing just as anyone else does, and it took me 12 months to see it.

You see, I waited there all those months for *Him* to heal me, and He was waiting on me to receive the healing He'd already provided. If you are waiting for Him to heal you, you're just wasting your time. However, if you will begin to *appropriate* your healing and *receive* that which He has already wrought for you — you will get it.

2 CORINTHIANS 5:1;6-8
1   For we know that if our earthly house of this tabernacle were dissolved, we have a building of God, an house not made with hands, eternal in the heavens.
6   Therefore we are always confident, knowing that, whilst we are at home in the body, we are absent from the Lord:
7   (For we walk by faith, not by sight:)
8   We are confident, I say, and willing rather to be absent from the body, and to be present with the Lord.

The body of man was made with hands, the inward man was not. When our body is put into the grave, we still have a building with God not made with hands.

Who is going to be absent from the body? *We* are (verse 6). Who is going to be present with the Lord? *We* are (verse 8). The Bible speaks of the inward man as being the real man — the real you.

> PHILIPPIANS 1:21-24
> 21 For to me to live is Christ, and to die is gain.
> 22 But if I [the inward man] live in the flesh [the body], this is the fruit of my labour: yet what I shall choose I wot not.
> 23 For I am in a strait betwixt two, having a desire to depart, and to be with Christ; which is far better:
> 24 Nevertheless to abide in the flesh is more needful for you.

Paul is saying here, "It's left up to me. I don't know whether I'm going to choose to go on living here for a while or to die."

Some people say, "Oh, that's all in the hands of God."

No! it's in *your* hands. *Many have missed it, thinking they were leaving it up to God as to whether or not they died, little realizing they were actually leaving it up to the devil. The devil is the author of death, not God.*

Paul died exactly when he wanted to die. He said, "I don't know which I am going to choose." He did not say, "I don't know what God's will is," or "I don't know what God is going to choose for me," or "I'm just praying that the will of the Lord be done."

No! That's where we miss it. Paul said, "I [the inward man] don't know whether I shall *choose* to stay here [in the flesh] a while or whether I shall *choose* to go on."

The inward man (the spirit) is the real man. God is a Spirit. He became a man, for Jesus was God manifested in the flesh living in a human body. He took on a physical body, yet when He did He was no less God than He was before He had a physical body. Even so, when man leaves his physical body at death, he is no less man than he was when he had his physical body. This was true of the rich man; it was true of the beggar Lazarus; it was true in my own experiences.

It is the inward man (the spirit) who contacts and knows God. We cannot know God through our human knowledge, through the mind. God is only revealed to man through the spirit. And when I say "through the spirit" I am not referring to the Holy Spirit, but to man's spirit. It is the spirit of man that contacts God, for God is a Spirit.

Jesus has a physical body — a flesh-and-bone body — but not flesh and *blood.* You recall that after His Resurrection He appeared to the disciples and they were frightened and supposed they had seen a spirit (a ghost). Jesus said to them, *"Handle me, and see; for a spirit hath not flesh and bones, as ye see me have"* (Luke 24:39). He asked them if they had any meat. They gave Him a piece of broiled fish and a honeycomb, and He ate it before them.

And then there was the time when Peter said, "I'm going fishing," and the others went with him. Suddenly they saw Jesus standing on the shore. He spoke to them and they went to Him. He had fish on the fire and He ate with them.

Yes, Jesus has a physical body right now — a resurrected, flesh-and-bone physical body.

God is a Spirit. (Notice that I did not say, "God is spirit." Some think God is spirit, and that that means He is a sort of impersonal influence. No, God is *a* Spirit.)

However, the fact that God is a Spirit does not mean that He has no shape or form in the spiritual realm, because He does.

Angels are spirits, the Bible says, and they have a form or a spirit body.

In the Old Testament, the prophet of God prophesied deliverance when the city was besieged, and everyone laughed at him because they were in starvation, hunger, and famine. Even his servant reprimanded him, so Elisha prayed, *"Lord, I pray thee, open his eyes, that he may see"* (2 Kings 6:17).

Elisha wasn't talking about his servant's physical eyes, but his spiritual eyes. When the eyes of his spirit were opened, he saw angels of fire, horses and chariots of fire all around the city!

And sometimes, as God wills, angels have the ability to take form or appearance in the material realm where we can see them — *but only as He wills.*

The Bible says that God talked to Moses face to face; so we know He has a face. A cloud was there, however, and Moses could not see God's face, for God said, *"Thou canst not see my face: for there shall no man see me, and live"* (Exod. 33:20).

And then God said, *". . .I will put thee in a clift of the rock, and will cover thee with my hand while I pass by: And I will take away mine hand, and thou shalt see my back parts . . . ."* (Exod. 33:22,23).

My point is this: God is a Spirit, yet He is no less real because He is a Spirit than He would be if He had a physical body. Jesus with His physical body in heaven now is not more real than the Holy Spirit, or God the Father.

Spiritual things are just as real as material — more real, in fact.

In First Peter 3:4 our spirit is called *"the hidden man of the heart."* The inward man, the spirit, is called "the hidden man." He is a man of the heart, of the spirit. He is hidden to the physical or the natural man. The natural man does not know he is there — but he is; and he is the real man.

In Romans 7:22 the spirit is called *"the inward man."* The terms "inward man" and "hidden man" give us God's definition of the human spirit.

Man is a spirit; he has a soul; and he lives in a body. With his *spirit*, man contacts the *spiritual* realm; with his *soul* he contacts the *intellectual and emotional* realm; and with his *body* he contacts the *physical* realm.

Chapter 4
What It Means To Believe with the Heart

*For with the heart man believeth unto righteous-
ness; and with the mouth confession is made unto
salvation.*

— Romans 10:10

We have established certain facts in the previous
chapter which we will summarize here.

When God speaks in His Word of the *heart,* He is not
speaking of the physical organ which pumps blood through
our bodies and keeps us alive. He is speaking of the human
spirit, which is the very center of man's being.

I've never forgotten a man whom I heard speak as a
youngster. (He called it preaching, but actually he was just
giving an intellectual discourse. It wasn't preaching
because it wasn't New Testament; it wasn't the Word of
God.)

His so-called sermon poked fun at those of us who
believe in old-fashioned, heart-felt salvation. He used the
term "heart" literally and said that if a man had a "change
of heart," he would have heart trouble and die.

This speaker thought that man was only mind and
body. But man is more than mind and body; he is spirit,
soul, and body. Man was created in the image and likeness
of God. Jesus said, *"God is a Spirit: and they that worship
him must worship him in spirit and in truth"* (John 4:24).

We have seen that the spirit of man is not his mind.
The mind is part of the soul's qualities. You can readily
identify the spirit if you speak with other tongues, because

43

this speaking comes from your heart, or out of your spirit.
Now you can see that *to believe God with your heart
means to believe God with your spirit, the inner man.*
In the previous chapter we referred to two Scriptures
which give us God's definition of the human spirit:

> **1 PETER 3:4**
> 4   But let it be the hidden man of the heart, in that which
> is not corruptible, even the ornament of a meek and quiet
> spirit, which is in the sight of God of great price.

> **ROMANS 7:22**
> 22 For I delight in the law of God after the inward man.

"The hidden man of the heart" is the spirit, the real
man. This real man, the hidden man, the inward man, is
spirit. He has a soul and he lives in a body.
With our spirit, we contact the spiritual realm.
With our soul, we contact the intellectual and emotional
realm.
With our body, we contact the physical realm.
You cannot contact God with your mind. You cannot
contact God with your body. *You can only contact God
with your spirit.*
And God contacts you through your spirit. When you
hear the Word of God preached, you hear it with your
physical ears. It then goes through your natural mind. But
if it is to affect you, you must receive it in your spirit.
Can you remember how the Word of God affected you
on the inside, in your spirit, before you were born again?
The Holy Spirit through the Word spoke to your heart,
or spirit.
Knowing that God contacts us through our spirits
helps us understand First Corinthians 2:14, *"But the*

natural man receiveth not the things of the Spirit of God: for they are foolishness unto him: neither can he know them, because they are spiritually discerned." (Another translation reads, "The natural man, or the natural mind, understandeth not the things of God ....")

The Word of God is of the Spirit of God, and it is foolish to the natural mind. You do not understand the Bible with your head; it is spiritually understood. You understand it with your heart!

You may have read certain chapters and verses many times, never understanding the meaning. Then one day you suddenly saw it. You said, "Why didn't I see that before?" It was because you now understood it with your heart.

You must receive the revelation of God's Word in your heart. That is why we have to depend on the Spirit of God to open and unveil the Word to us.

MARK 11:23,24
23 For verily I say unto you, That whosoever shall say unto this mountain, Be thou removed, and be thou cast into the sea; and shall not doubt in his heart, but shall believe that those things which he saith shall come to pass; he shall have whatsoever he saith.
24 Therefore I say unto you, What things soever ye desire, when ye pray, believe that ye receive them, and ye shall have them.

For almost the entire 16 months I was bedfast, I tried to figure out what was meant by, *"What things soever ye desire, when ye pray, believe that ye receive them, and ye shall have them."*

First of all, the devil told me that it doesn't mean what it says. He told me, "Now that doesn't mean what things soever ye desire naturally, or physically, or materially, such as healing. (My desire was for healing.) That just means what things soever ye desire spiritually."

I am sorry I even listened to the devil, for if Mark 11:24 doesn't mean what it says, then Jesus told a lie. However, I didn't know that then, so I decided to send for my pastor to ask him what the Scripture meant.

My grandmother contacted him and he said that he couldn't make it the next day but would be there the day after that. When he asked what time would be best to come, my grandmother said, "Kenneth is at his best in the mornings. If you could come around 8:30 it would be best, because after 10 o'clock he lies in a sort of stupor and I don't know if he could understand what you were saying."

He said he would be there, but thank God he never showed up. At the time, I wept when he didn't come, because I had great confidence in my pastor, and I was certain he would know what the Bible meant here. However, after I received my healing and went back to the same church, I found out what he thought. He said, "The poor boy stayed in bed so long it affected his mind."

(According to his reasoning, wouldn't it be wonderful if we could get more minds affected? As soon as my mind was "affected," as he put it, my paralysis left. As soon as my mind was "affected," my heart condition left, and I was healed and raised up.)

It was a good thing he didn't come, because at that time I would have believed what he said.

My grandmother walked across town to ask another minister of the same denomination to come. He said that he would, but thank God he never showed up either.

Again I wept, but now I am thoroughly convinced that God prevented them from coming to see me, because I would have believed what they said.

Finally, my aunt, who belonged to another denomination, said that her pastor would come to see me. I didn't much believe he would, but one day he did. My heart leaped for joy within me when he came in. Doctors allowed only one person at a time in the room, so no one else came in with him.

My range of sight was just a few inches away from my face, but I could hear him coming. Suddenly, as he stooped over me, I could see his face. He took my hand in his.

With difficulty, I tried to speak. My throat was partially paralyzed, and my tongue didn't work right. I was trying to ask him to get my New Testament and read Mark 11:24 and tell me if it meant what it said. (Isn't it strange that you should have to ask somebody if Jesus meant what He said?)

I was struggling to get the words out. If he had waited long enough, eventually I would have, but before I could get going on what I was trying to say, he patted the back of my hand, put on his professional voice, and said, "Just be patient, my boy. In a few more days it will *all* be over."

It was dark in that room. He laid my hand down on my chest, turned around, and walked out. I hadn't gotten one intelligible word over to him, and he had extinguished the only hope I had — just as if a light in the room had been turned off.

Normally, I couldn't hear very well, but I think the devil let me hear extra well that day. As this pastor went into the next room and the family gathered around him, I could hear him pray, "Our Father: We pray that You would help this grandmother and grandfather who are about to be bereaved of this grandson."

At that, something rose up inside me. I couldn't holler out loud, but I was like the mischievous little boy whose teacher made him stand in the corner. He said, "I may be standing up on the outside, but inside I'm sitting down." Inside I literally yelled out, "I ain't dead yet!"

And then he prayed, "Bless this dear mother. Prepare her heart for this hour of darkness which is about to overtake her." Again, on the inside I yelled, "I ain't dead yet!"

He left. But he had knocked all the props out from under me and had put out all the lights. For more than a month, I didn't even look at the Bible.

Finally, when I did pick up the Bible, I turned to Mark 11:24 and said, "Dear Lord Jesus, I am going to take this Scripture for what it says. And if You didn't lie about it, I'm coming off this bed. If I don't get off this bed, it will be because the Son of God told a falsehood and I'll just have them throw away the New Testament."

But it was still 11 more months before I came off that bed. I would think about that Scripture, meditate on it, and pray. Then I would look to see if God had healed me. I would feel my arms and legs, but I wasn't healed yet; I still was paralyzed.

The Word is spiritually understood. The Word is of the Spirit of God. Holy men of old wrote as they were moved by the Holy Spirit.

On the second Tuesday of August 1934, at 8:30 in the morning, as I meditated on that Scripture, I finally understood what it said. The light came. It was as if someone had turned on a light inside me.

I tell people the meaning of this verse over and over

again, yet I know they must understand it with their spirit
to see it. However, I must keep repeating it, because the
more the meaning is shared, the more people catch on. I
can tell when it dawns on them, because their eyes light
up. Others will just sit there staring, but more and more
catch on all the time.

"What things soever ye desire" means exactly what
it says.

"When ye pray" means right then — the moment you
pray.

"Believe that ye receive them and ye shall have them"
in common, everyday language means, "You've got to
believe you've got it before you get it."

When I understood it, I immediately said, "Why, Lord,
I see what I've got to do. I must believe *while I am still
lying here* flat on my back, that the paralysis is healed."
(Notice I said "is healed," not "going to be healed." Many
people would say, "I believe God is *going to heal* me." But
that is not New Testament believing. I know, because I
had stayed in that bed for a year believing that and never
got anything.)

Notice that it says, *"believe that ye receive them, and
ye shall have them."* You believe it first, and then you will
have it.

(Someone said, "I don't understand it." You can't
understand it with your head. The things of the Spirit of
God are foolishness unto the natural mind and the Bible
is of the Spirit of God. The Scriptures are spiritually
discerned. You have to understand it with your *spirit*.)

The moment I understood this verse, I began to act
on the Word. *There is always some way you can act on
the Word.* The only way I could act on it at that moment

was to raise my hands and praise God for His Word. I said, "Thank God, I believe. I believe that my paralysis is healed. I believe my body is well."

"... *Believe* [first] *that ye receive them* [the desires], *and ye shall have them* [the desires] " (Mark 11:24). *The Amplified Bible's* translation reads, "For this reason I am telling you, whatever you ask for in prayer, believe — trust and be confident — that it is granted to you, and you will [get it]." When are you going to get it? After you trust and are confident it is granted to you.

Too many want to get it first and *then* they will believe they have it. But Jesus said that you have to believe you've got it, and then you will have it.

You believe it with your heart. And to believe with the heart means to believe with the spirit. How is it that our spirit obtains faith which our intellect cannot obtain? The answer is through the Word of God.

Matthew 4:4 says, *"Man shall not live by bread alone, but by every word that proceedeth out of the mouth of God."* Jesus is speaking here of spiritual food. He is using a natural, human term to convey a spiritual thought. Our spirits become filled with assurance and confidence as we meditate in the Word. The Word is spiritual food; it is faith food. The Word is the food that builds the spirit. The Word of God is the food that makes the spirit strong and gives it quiet assurance.

To believe with the heart means to believe apart from what your physical body or your physical senses may tell you. The body — the physical man — believes what he sees with the physical eye, hears with the physical ear, or what his physical feelings tell him. The spirit, or the heart, however, believes what the Word says, regardless of seeing, hearing, or feeling.

Faith must be based upon what the Word says. Many people are prayed for again and again and again. (Now I do not mean that you should not come back to be prayed for the second time. I have reference to those who come repeatedly.) Those who come repeatedly and do not receive healing do not have faith in the Word. They have a natural human faith. Because they do not see that they are healed or have some physical evidence of it, they won't believe it.

Heart faith believes the Word of God first; then the physical evidence will take care of itself.

To believe with all your heart is to believe with your spirit. To believe with all your heart is to believe independently of your head and of your body.

Proverbs 3:5 tells us, *"Trust in the Lord with all thine heart; and lean not unto thine own understanding."* Most people practice that, all right, but they practice it in reverse. They trust with all their understanding and lean not to their own heart!

The next two verses in Proverbs 3 say, *"In all thy ways acknowledge him, and he shall direct thy paths. Be not wise in thine own eyes...."* (vv. 6,7). In other words, "Don't be wise with natural human knowledge, which would cause you to act independently of the Word of God."

In the New Testament we find the counterpart to this Scripture: *"(For the weapons of our warfare are not carnal, but mighty through God to the pulling down of strong holds;) Casting down imaginations [reasonings], and every high thing that exalteth itself against the knowledge of God, and bringing into captivity every thought to the obedience of Christ"* (2 Cor. 10:4,5).

Just after I walked off the bed of sickness, I went back

to high school. Standing more than 6 feet tall, I weighed only 89 pounds. They called me "the walking skeleton."

One day the principal called me into his office and said, "Do you think you should come to school? The lady teachers are worried that you might fall dead in the classroom. They have called Dr. Robason, and he has said that it is entirely possible. In fact, I called the doctor myself and he said you didn't have any business walking two miles to school and climbing steps. He said that you were up by sheer willpower and he would give you 90 days at the most to live. So do you think it wise to come to school?"

"Sir," I answered, "I am not up by willpower. I'm going by faith. The Lord Jesus Christ, when He was on earth, said in Mark 11:24, *'Therefore I say unto you, What things soever ye desire, when ye pray, believe that ye receive them, and ye shall have them.'* I believe that I have received healing for my heart and my body; and I am not walking by willpower, I am walking by faith."

That man began to weep. He said, "Son, if that is what you are doing, even though I don't understand it myself, I wouldn't stand in your way a minute. Come to school if you want to. I'll talk to the teachers."

"I believe I have what I prayed for," I said to him, "I believe I have what I asked."

"I wouldn't put one stone in your way," he went on. "I phoned your mother about taking you out and she told me the same thing. She said that you were not up by willpower but by faith, and that your faith would hold."

"It will, sir," I said.

But then, without realizing it, he played right into the hands of the enemy. He did put some stones in my way.

He said, "I'm going to talk to your teachers, and any time you want to, you may go out of class for a breath of fresh air or a drink of water. You have my permission to go home anytime you need to. You won't have to ask anybody anything. Just do whatever you feel like doing."

Yes, he made it easy to fail. But if I had missed one class, or failed to climb the steps once, I would have been admitting failure. So I didn't miss a class. And, weak as I was, by the time the afternoon classes rolled around, it would have been easy to do so.

I can tell you that the devil is a good mathematician. My worst struggles came in the night. Just after I would get into bed, the devil would say, "Well, boy, you've just got 'so many' days left. Remember what Dr. Robason said: 'Only 90 days.' " Each night he would tell me exactly how many days were left.

Sometimes for hours in the night I would struggle, casting down imaginations. It's not always easy, but, thank God, it can be done. "*Casting down imaginations, and every high thing that exalteth itself against the knowledge of God, and bringing into captivity every thought to the obedience of Christ*" (2 Cor. 10:5). This simply means to bring every thought into captivity to the obedience of the Word, for the Word is Christ. So I would begin to think in line with what His Word says.

"Now, Mr. Devil," I would say, "I appreciate Dr. Robason highly. I appreciate him more than any of my five doctors. He sat down by my bedside one day and told me the truth. He told me that there was nothing that could be done by any doctor, and that unless a Higher Power intervened, there was no hope. (However, it is not a matter of a Higher Power intervening, it is a matter of your believing God.)

"I appreciate the fact that he has never charged us a penny and that he would come anytime we called him, but I am not going by what he said. I am walking in the light of the Word. And the Word says that God heard me, and I am healed. The Word says that I have been healed, and I believe the Word."

This is very important: If you want to walk by faith, the Word must be superior to anything and everything else. It must be superior to any knowledge, whether that knowledge is yours or someone else's.

When you trust God with all your heart, a quietness and a peace come into your spirit, because the Word says, *"For we which have believed do enter into rest...."* (Heb. 4:3).

We take God at His Word when we see that He says, *"But my God shall supply all your need according to his riches in glory by Christ Jesus"* (Phil. 4:19). We simply know in our spirits that everything we need will be supplied, and we don't worry. We have no anxiety. (If we were worrying and being anxious, we would not be believing.)

Our hearts take courage as we read the Word. As we meditate in this Word, our assurance becomes deeper. This assurance in our spirit is independent of our human reasoning or human knowledge. It may contradict human reasoning. It even may contradict physical evidence. Believing God with the heart means to believe apart from your body.

Coming out of church one night, rather than walking down the steps, I jumped into the yard. My foot hit a rut in the ground, my ankle turned, and I fell. My ankle popped like a gun going off, and it seemed to be broken.

I couldn't touch it to the ground, so I hopped on one foot over to the parsonage.

As I answered my wife's question as to what had happened, I could see that the ankle was swollen and seemed to be in bad shape.

But I began to recall what the Word of God says, so I called God's attention to the fact that my eye could see and my physical senses told me that it could be broken. I could certainly feel the pain and throbbing. Then I called God's attention and the devil's attention to the fact that the Word of God says that I am healed. (Some people who are walking in the natural rather than in the spirit — even Spirit-filled Christians — sometimes will think you rather strange, but they will just have to think it.) The next day, I drove my car almost 100 miles. God had healed me.

A certain minister's testimony was told to me several times before I heard it from him firsthand. Playing baseball at a youth camp, he slid into third base and broke his ankle. Part of the bone was sticking out through the skin.

As some were preparing to get him into town to a doctor, one of the ministers asked him if he wanted medical help or for God to heal him. When he said that he would rather have his healing, the minister said, "All right, you can. I have been in the Pentecostal Movement from the beginning," and he began to tell him about broken bones he had seen healed.

For 40 minutes, he sat there by third base, talking to the injured man, getting his mind off the ankle and foot. Then he told him to get up. But the minute he put his broken foot on the ground, he fainted and fell.

The counseling minister worked to revive him, talked

with him another 40 minutes, then helped him up on his
good foot. However, when weight was put on the injured
foot, again the wounded man fainted.

The older minister said to him when he again revived,
"We're missing it somewhere." So the older minister asked
the Lord, "God, where are we missing it?" Then the
minister said, "Oh, I see. I see it now. Son, this time when
you get up, don't get up on your good foot. Get up on your
bad one." When he did, instantly he was healed! There was
no pain at all!

Believing with your heart is independent of your sense
knowledge.

Dr. Lilian B. Yeomans knew what faith was. In one of
her books, which are some of the best you can read on healing, she says, "God delights in His children stepping out
over the aching void with nothing under their feet but the
Word of God." Again she said, "To look to see whether
God is healing you is a sin."

Dr. Yeomans was a medical doctor who received healing and deliverance from a hopeless dependence on nar-
cotics and then devoted the rest of her life to preaching
and teaching divine healing.

A minister who had been a student in one of her classes
in a Bible college told me of this incident. She was in the
habit of praying for students in the classroom, and held
healing services in her classes. It seems he went up and
requested prayer.

"What for?" she asked.

"I want you to pray for my cold," he answered.

"Your cold? Well, if it is *your* cold there's no use in
praying. You have already accepted it and you won't get
any healing. Now if you want to be delivered from the

devil's cold, then we'll pray."
   "Oh, that's what I meant," he said.
   She replied, "Say what you mean."

Chapter 5
How To Train the Human Spirit

*The spirit of man is the candle of the Lord,
searching all the inward parts of the belly.*
— Proverbs 20:27

Your spirit can be educated just as your mind can be. And your spirit can be built up in strength just as your body can be.

Here are four rules by which the human spirit can be trained and developed:

1. By meditating in the Word.
2. By practicing the Word.
3. By giving the Word first place.
4. By instantly obeying the voice of your spirit.

After a while you can know the will of God the Father in all the minor details of life, because it is through your spirit, and not through your mind or reasoning faculties, that He communicates with you.

When God says in Proverbs 20:27 that the spirit of man is the candle of the Lord, He means that He is going to use man's own spirit to enlighten and guide him.

1. Meditating in the Word
Three of these four points have to do with the Word of God. We must realize the value of God's Word and the value of quiet meditation in the Word.

The most deeply spiritual men and women I know give time to meditation in the Word of God. You cannot develop spiritual wisdom without meditation. God made that fact

59

known to Joshua at the very beginning of Joshua's
ministry, just after the death of Moses.

JOSHUA 1:8
**8　This book of the law shall not depart out of thy mouth;
but thou shalt meditate therein day and night, that thou
mayest observe to do according to all that is written
therein: for then thou shalt make thy way prosperous, and
then thou shalt have good success.**

Another translation of the last phrase reads, "and then
you will be able to deal wisely in the things of life." God
told Joshua that if he would meditate in the Word, his way
would be prosperous and he would have good success.

I taught along this line at a ministerial convention, and
a minister who attended gave me this report later. He said
that he had been doing everything he could to make a success of his church. He said that if he heard of a pastor who
was doing well, he visited him, watched what he did, and
studied the kind of program he had. Then he would try
to put that man's program into action in his own church,
but it never worked. He had flown all over the country
doing this.

Then he decided to follow the rule God gave Joshua.
He decided he would meditate in the way I had taught,
taking a little time out each morning.

After 30 days of praying this way, not asking much,
but just waiting and meditating on the Word, one Sunday
they had a landslide. More people were saved there that
day than had been in the previous two or three years. His
people were revived, and he began to have good success.

That was *his* life and that was where *he* needed to have
good success. *Your* life's calling is something else. But it

is certainly true that *your* way can be prosperous also, and you can have good success. You can know how to deal wisely in the affairs of life.

Take time to meditate in God's Word. Shut yourself in alone with your own spirit, with the world shut out. Begin by taking 10 or 15 minutes daily for meditation; that isn't much. Begin the development of your own spirit. Begin — and then it will grow. Begin *taking time.*

2. Practicing the Word
Practicing the Word means being a "doer of the Word," as we are told in the book of James.

> **JAMES 1:22**
> 22 But be ye doers of the word, and not hearers only....

We have many "talkers about the Word," and even many "rejoicers about the Word," but we don't have many "doers of the Word."

Begin to practice being a "doer of the Word" by doing in all circumstances what the Word tells you to do.

Some have thought that being a "doer of the Word" means to keep the Ten Commandments. That is not what James 1:22 is talking about. After all, we, under the New Covenant, have but one commandment: the commandment of love. Jesus said, *"A new commandment I give unto you, That ye love one another; as I have loved you, that ye also love one another"* (John 13:34).

A "doer of the Word" will do that. If you love someone, you won't steal from him. You won't lie about him. Paul said that love is the fulfilling of the law. If you walk in love, you won't break any law which was given to curb sin.

Being a "doer of the Word" means that we are to do
primarily what is written in the epistles. They are the letters written to us, the Church.

As an example of doing the Word, let us look at some
instructions given us in one of the epistles.

PHILIPPIANS 4:6
6 Be careful for nothing; but in every thing by prayer and
supplication with thanksgiving let your requests be made
known unto God.

We don't mind practicing part of this — the part that
says to pray. But if you practice just that part and not
the first part, you are not practicing the Word. You are
not a "doer of the Word."

The *Amplified* translation of Philippians 4:6 begins,
"Do not fret or have any anxiety about anything . . . ."
First we are told not to fret. If you fret and have anxieties,
it isn't going to do any good to make requests. That kind
of praying doesn't work. An over-anxious prayer full of
fretfulness doesn't work.

I felt very sorry for a minister who came to me some
time ago. But sometimes it doesn't give a man the answer
just to sympathize with him. Storms and tests were in his
life. His stomach was upset; he wasn't able to keep
anything down that he ate. He couldn't sleep, and his
nerves were shot because of a particular incident.

He came to me for help. I began to tell him what the
Word said and how to pray about it. When I encouraged
him to take this Scripture we have just read and to *do it,*
he rebelled and said, "Oh, yes, but everybody doesn't have
the faith that you have."

I told him then that it was not a matter of having a

lot of faith, but a matter of endeavoring to practice the Word. I told him that if he would practice the Word, his faith would be built up. And I told him how I practice this particular verse. (When I get alone, I read this verse aloud. I tell the Lord that His Word is true and that I believe it.)

I told that minister that he would be tempted to say he couldn't help worrying and fretting, but God has not asked us to do something we cannot do. When God said not to fret, that means we can keep from it. God is a just God, and He will not ask us to do something we cannot do.

When I first began practicing this verse, it was easy to believe that I could make my requests known unto God, but it was hard to believe that I could not fret. However, since God says that we don't have to fret, I would say, "I refuse to fret or have any anxiety about anything."

I tell the Lord that I bring my requests unto Him and then I thank Him for the answer. This quiets my spirit and pacifies the troubled attitude the devil tries to make me have.

Then I get up and go about my business, but before you know it, the devil is trying to get me again. I simply go right back and read this verse and keep claiming it.

The minister began to practice this. He told me later the problem was worked out and did not get as big as he had expected. He was being sued over a certain matter, but it did not amount to anything. God helped him out of it all.

You can become so fretful over something that you can't eat or sleep. Your stomach feels as though it has butterflies in it. But all you have to do is practice the Word and you will get results. Philippians 4:7 is a result of practicing Philippians 4:6.

PHILIPPIANS 4:7
7 And the peace of God, which passeth all understanding, shall keep your hearts and minds through Christ Jesus.

Many people want what the seventh verse talks about, but they don't want to practice what the sixth verse says to do to get it. The *Amplified* translation of the seventh verse says, "And God's peace . . . which transcends all understanding, shall garrison and mount guard over your hearts and minds in Christ Jesus." God's peace will keep guard over your heart and your mind. But can you reap the results and have the peace without being a "doer of the Word"? No, you really cannot.

The sixth verse tells us not to fret. People who worry and fret continually think on the wrong side of life. Verse 8 tells us what we are to think about:

PHILIPPIANS 4:8
8 Finally, brethren, whatsoever things are true, whatsoever things are honest, whatsoever things are just, whatsoever things are pure, whatsoever things are lovely, whatsoever things are of good report; if there be any virtue, and if there be any praise, think on these things.

DO verse 8. Practice this verse. Think about the right things. Many people think about the wrong things. And you know what they are thinking about because of what they talk about. The Bible says, *"out of the abundance of the heart, the mouth speaketh."* They continually worry, fret, and think on the wrong side of life, and they continually talk unbelief. You cannot be a "doer of the Word" and continue to talk unbelief. The more you talk about some things, the bigger they get. If something does not meet all these qualifications — true, honest, just, pure, lovely, etc. — don't think about it and don't talk about it.

The *Amplified* translation of First Corinthians 13:7 reads, "Love . . . is ever ready to believe the best of every person." I have found through the years that most of the stories I have heard about people don't even meet the first qualification; they aren't true. So don't talk about the stories you hear — don't even think about them. Some of the things you hear might be true, but they might not be pure and lovely (and notice this) and of a good report. Therefore we are not to think about them.

By thinking about these things, we give place to the devil. His greatest weapon is the power of suggestion. He is ever endeavoring to enter your thought life. That is why we are instructed in God's Word, "think on these things."

God the Holy Spirit speaks to the Church particularly in the epistles. Meditate on what He has to say in these letters to the Church and be a "doer of the Word." You will grow spiritually.

3. Giving the Word First Place

The training, development, and education of our spirits comes by giving the Word of God first place in our lives.

PROVERBS 4:20-22
20 My son, attend to my words; incline thine ear unto my sayings.
21 Let them not depart from thine eyes; keep them in the midst of thine heart.
22 For they are life unto those that find them, and health to all their flesh.

God says in this passage, "*attend to my words* [give heed to them — put them first] ; *incline thine ear unto my*

sayings [listen to what I have to say]. *Let them not depart
from thine eyes* [keep looking at the Word of God]; *keep
them* [my words] . . .*in your heart."*

There are rich dividends for doing this. Why is it that
God tells us to put His words first, to listen to what He
has to say, to keep looking at His Word, and to keep His
Word in our heart? It is because "they [His words] are *life*
unto those that find them, and *health* to all their flesh."
(The margin of the *King James* reads, "and *medicine* to
all their flesh.")

Notice that there is healing in the Word. It is strange
to me that some people won't put God's Word first in this
area. In the 12 years I pastored, there were members who
would get sick, go to the hospital, and ask for prayer
afterwards.

I am not saying that it is wrong to have a doctor, certainly not. We believe in hospitals and doctors and thank
God for them. But I am saying why not put God's Word
first? Sometimes Christians turn to the Word as a last
resort.

A Baptist minister who didn't particularly believe in
divine healing at the time, told how he had had problems
with his tonsils. His doctor kept telling him that they must
be removed, so the date was set.

Each morning he and his wife would read the Bible and
pray with the children before school. On the very date he
was scheduled to enter the hospital, their Scripture
passage was the one which tells of King Asa who got a
disease in his feet, and instead of seeking the Lord, he
sought physicians and died.

The minister said that he was struck by this. He realized that he hadn't even prayed about his tonsils. He

shared this with his wife and children and asked that they pray together about his tonsils.

When they prayed, the Lord told him not to have them removed. To his astonishment, the Lord healed the tonsils and he has had no more trouble with them.

There is a lesson to be learned here. The Bible does not imply that King Asa died because he put the physicians first. However, it does imply that he should have put the Lord first. We should train ourselves to put the Lord first.

We should train ourselves to ask concerning any matter, "What does God's Word have to say about this?" We should ask ourselves what God has to say about *anything* that may come up in our life — and then put that Word first.

Sometimes family and friends will try to rush you into things, but you need to think about what the Word of God says. Put God's Word first in every area of life.

4. Instantly Obeying the Voice of Your Spirit

The human spirit has a voice. We call that voice "conscience." Sometimes we call it "intuition," "an inner voice," or "guidance." The world calls it "a hunch." What it is, is your spirit speaking to you. Every man's spirit, whether he is saved or unsaved, has a voice.

The human spirit, as we have seen in the previous chapters, is a spiritual man, a spirit man, an inward and hidden man. He is hidden to the physical senses. You cannot see him with the physical eyes or touch him with your physical hands.

This is the man who has become a new creature in Christ according to Second Corinthians 5:17. When a man is born again, his spirit is reborn.

God prophesied through both Ezekiel and Jeremiah that a time would come when He would take the old stony heart out of men and put in a new one. He said that He would put His Spirit in us. Under the New Covenant, the New Birth becomes available.

The New Birth is a rebirth of the human spirit. As Second Corinthians 5:17 tells us, if any man is in Christ, he is a new creature — everything that was old in his spirit — the old nature — is taken away and all things become new.

As you give this newborn spirit the privilege of meditating on the Word of God, this becomes the source of its information. Your spirit will become strong, and the inward voice of your conscience, educated in the spirit, will become a true guide, for *"The spirit of man is the candle of the Lord."* Your newborn spirit has within it the life and nature of God.

The Holy Spirit dwells within your spirit. *"Greater is he that is in you, than he that is in the world"* (1 John 4:4). The Holy Spirit dwells within you — not in your head, but in your spirit. God has to communicate with you through your spirit because that is where He is. Your spirit gets its information through Him. *Learn to obey your spirit!*

Some say that conscience is not a safe guide, but that statement is not always true. The conscience is a safe guide in the believer. Your conscience is the voice of your spirit; and the voice of your spirit can become the voice of God speaking to you. God uses your spirit to enlighten and guide you. And as your spirit has the privilege of meditating and feeding upon the Word of God, it increasingly becomes a safe guide. It is trained in the Word. Paul said that he always obeyed his conscience.

Sometimes people say, "Well, you are a minister, so the Holy Spirit would speak to you differently than He would to me."

No, He deals with us in ministering and enables us to minister a little differently, but in speaking to us as individuals about our own lives He deals with us just as He deals with all believers. He speaks to us with this inward voice — the voice of our own spirit speaking — not with just the voice of the Holy Spirit.

We miss it by not always looking to the spiritual. Instead, we try to get God to come over into the sense, or physical, realm. We put out a *fleece* and tell God, "You do this if You want me to do that."

Gideon put out a fleece, but remember he didn't have the Spirit of God. In the Old Testament the Holy Spirit only came "upon" certain ones to minister. Gideon was what we would call a lay member. He did not have the anointing of the Holy Spirit. God had to deal with him through the senses. And God might do that today, but if He has to, it is because we are spiritually dull!

Under the New Testament, Jesus said, "*And I will pray the Father, and he shall give you another Comforter, that he may abide with you for ever*" (John 14:16). Gideon didn't know the Holy Spirit; you know Him.

God deals with man through his human spirit, by the Holy Spirit. And Jesus said of Him, "*when he, the Spirit of truth, is come, he will guide you into all truth . . . .*" (John 16:13).

Satan is the god of the sense realm. (See Second Corinthians 4:4.) And many times people try to get God to move in the sense realm.

Nowhere in the New Testament does it say, "As many

as are led by fleeces, they are the sons of God." But you will find that the Bible does say, *"For as many as are led by the Spirit of God, they are the sons of God"* (Rom. 8:14).

God will lead and guide you through your own spirit. You need to know that. *"The spirit of man is the candle of the Lord...."* Too many miss it because they are not taking advantage of what belongs to them.

One businessman told me he lost several thousand dollars because he got involved in a business deal when a fleece he had put out made it look as though he should. His home and more than one business were paid for. Someone came along with what sounded like a good business deal. He didn't have the necessary cash on hand and would have to mortgage his property to borrow the money. He told the man who had presented the deal that he would have to pray about it.

"Well, we will have to do something in just a couple of days," he was told, "or this opportunity will be gone."

So he put out a fleece to the effect of, "Lord, if You want me to do this, You do something here in this natural realm."

Well, the fleece said yes, so he followed the fleece, and lost all his money.

After hearing me teach along these lines, he told me of the incident and said he had been confused and wondered where he had missed God. But now he remembered that *all the time an inward voice was telling him not to do it!*

We need to realize that God will guide us through our spirits. If our spirit has the life and nature of God in it and has the privilege to meditate in the Word of God, our spirit becomes a safe guide.

In the earlier days of my ministry, I had heard people talking about putting out fleeces, so I put one out regarding accepting the pastorate of a church. My fleece said that I should leave the church where I was and take the other one. Well, let me tell you — *I got fleeced.* I learned it didn't work. God has a better way than a hit-and-miss system.

That was the only time I ever missed God in changing churches. The other times I prayed and listened to the inward voice and obeyed my own spirit. When I did, I operated in the perfect will of God.

Learn to obey the voice of your spirit. If you are not used to doing that, of course, you won't get there quickly. In the beginning of this chapter we said that your spirit could be *educated* as your mind could be, and your spirit could be built up and strengthened as your body could be. But just as you did not begin school in the first grade one week and graduate from the 12th grade the next, your spirit will not be educated or trained overnight.

As you walk in the light of the Word and put into practice the four rules listed in this chapter, you eventually will come to the place where you will know in your spirit what you should do in even the minor details of life. You will receive guidance and will always instantly get either a "yes" or a "no."

"The spirit of man is the candle of the Lord, searching all the inward parts of the belly."

Chapter 6
How To Write Your Own Ticket with God

And a certain woman, which had an issue of blood twelve years,

And had suffered many things of many physicians, and had spent all that she had, and was nothing bettered, but rather grew worse,

When she had heard of Jesus, came in the press behind, and touched his garment.

For she said, If I may touch but his clothes, I shall be whole.

And straightway the fountain of her blood was dried up; and she felt in her body that she was healed of that plague.

And Jesus, immediately knowing in himself that virtue had gone out of him, turned him about in the press, and said, Who touched my clothes?

And his disciples said unto him, Thou seest the multitude thronging thee, and sayest thou, Who touched me?

And he looked round about to see her that had done this thing.

But the woman fearing and trembling, knowing what was done in her, came and fell down before him, and told him all the truth.

And he said unto her, Daughter, thy faith hath made thee whole; go in peace, and be whole of thy plague.

— Mark 5:25-34

One night as some friends were preparing to serve refreshments after a service in Phoenix, Arizona, I had an unusually strong urge from the Holy Spirit to pray.

"I *have* to pray. I *must* pray. I have *got* to pray now," I told my friends.

"Let's just all pray, then," they agreed.

My knees had hardly touched the floor until I was in the Spirit. Do you know what it means to be in the Spirit? You become more conscious of spiritual things than you are of your natural surroundings. John was in the Spirit on the Lord's Day (Rev. 1:10).

At that moment I didn't know I was in Phoenix, or even in that room. It seemed as if I knelt in a white cloud.

For 45 minutes I prayed in tongues, with groanings, as hard and fast as I could. I knew that I was interceding for someone who was lost. At the end of that time of intercession, I had a note of victory.

Then I had a vision. The Lord showed me a detailed vision of a 72-year-old man who was going to be saved in the coming Sunday night service.

Then the Lord Jesus Himself appeared to me. I saw Him as clearly as I would see you. He stood within three feet of me. He discussed things concerning my ministry and finances, and He even discussed things concerning our United States government. All of these things came to pass just as He said they would. He concluded by exhorting me, "Be faithful and fulfill thy ministry, my son, for the time is short." This vision took place in December 1953.

Jesus turned around to walk away, and I said, "Dear Lord Jesus, before You go, may I please ask You a question?"

He retraced His steps, stood close to where I was kneeling, and said, "You may."

I said, "Dear Lord, I have two sermons I preach concerning the woman who touched Your clothes and was healed when You were on earth. I received both of these sermons by inspiration. I preach them everywhere I go. And every time I preach them, I seem to be conscious in my spirit that the Holy Spirit is trying to get another sermon from this fifth chapter of Mark to me — a sermon that would complement the first two.

"Then, at times of prayer when I have a great anointing," I said, "I will come to the place where it seems I am going to receive that message into my spirit, but somehow or other, I fail to. If I am right about this, I wish You would give me that sermon."

He said, "You are correct. My Spirit, the Holy Spirit, has endeavored to get another sermon into your spirit, but you have failed to pick it up. While I am here, I will do what you ask. I will give you that sermon outline. Now get your pencil and paper and write it down."

I opened my eyes to ask for paper and pencil. I didn't see Jesus any longer; I saw the people who were praying with me. When I closed my eyes, there Jesus stood as before. This was a spiritual vision.

There are three types of visions: (1) *a spiritual vision,* when you see with the eyes of your spirit; (2) *a trance,* when your physical senses are suspended, and you do not know at that moment that you have a body; and (3) what I call *an open vision,* the highest type of vision, when your physical senses are all intact. You are not in a trance. Your eyes are wide open, yet you see into the spirit realm.

I am not smart enough to have figured all of this out. One time when Jesus appeared to me in a vision, He told me there are three kinds of visions. He explained them to me and proved them with Scriptures. But you do not have to accept this just because I said so. Do not accept anything anyone tells you just because they had a vision if it cannot be proved by the Word of God.

If Jesus tells you anything — if the Spirit of God brings any revelation to you — it must be in line with the Bible, or it is not from the Spirit of God. Holy men of old wrote the Scripture as they were moved by the Holy Spirit (2 Peter 1:21), and the Holy Spirit is not going to contradict Himself, or make Himself out a liar.

Jesus said, "Write down: 1,2,3,4." With my eyes shut, I wrote down 1,2,3,4. I knew the sermon had four points.

He said, *"If anybody, anywhere, will take these four steps or put these four principles into operation, he will always receive whatever he wants from Me or from God the Father."*

I need to explain here that these four steps He gave me can be put into operation immediately, and you can receive anything in the present tense, such as salvation, the baptism of the Holy Spirit, healing for your body, spiritual victory, or finances. Anything that the Bible promises you now, you can receive now by taking these four steps.

However, some things, such as some financial needs and the manifestation of some healings, etc., may take time to develop. Then the four steps become principles that you must put into practice over a period of time. (A farmer cannot go out tomorrow and start picking cotton or threshing wheat until it has had time to grow.) But, thank God, whether they are steps to be taken immediately, or principles to be practiced over time, you can have what you say.

You can write your own ticket with God.
Jesus said, "Step 1: Say it."

It is so simple it almost seems foolish. Every one of
the four steps is simple. After all, Jesus, in all of His
preaching, never brought out anything very complicated.
Did you ever notice that? He talked in terms that even
the uneducated could understand, because few of the people
He preached to had the advantage of an education.

Jesus talked about vineyards and orchards, sheepfolds
and shepherds. He illustrated spiritual verities in such a
simple way that the common people could understand him.
God never gives anybody anything so complicated that
it cannot be understood. If it comes from the Father, it
will be clear, concise, and simple.

We think sometimes that Jesus always initiated healings on His own, that the people had nothing to do with
it. We may not stop to think that the people then, as now,
had something to do with it; they had their part to play.
What if the blind man had not washed the clay off his eyes
in the pool of Siloam (John 9)? Would he have seen? No,
he would not have seen. What about the man lying by the
pool of Bethesda (John 5)? What if he had said, "I can't
get up!" Did he have any part to play? Yes, he did!

Jesus asked me this question: "What was the first step
the woman with the issue of blood took toward receiving
her healing?"

The Bible says that someone had told her about Jesus
(Mark 5:27). She knew about Jesus. She knew He was healing people. The 28th verse tells us, *"For SHE SAID, If
I may touch but his clothes, I shall be whole."* That is the
first thing she did: *She said.*

In my vision, Jesus said, "Positive or negative, it is
up to the individual. According to what the individual

says, that shall he receive."

He said, "This woman could have made a negative confession instead of a positive one, and that would have been
what she received. She could have said, 'There's no use
for me to go. I've suffered so long. Twelve years I've been
sick. All the best doctors have given up on my case. I've
spent all of my living upon physicians. I'm not better, but
growing worse. I have nothing to live for. I might as well
die.' "

He said, "If that had been what she said, that would
have been what she received. But she did not speak
negatively. She spoke positively. For she said, 'If I may
touch but his clothes, I shall be whole.' " And it came to
pass!

For you can have what you say. **You can write your
own ticket with God.** And the first step in writing your
own ticket with God is: *Say it.*

There are two parts to everything you receive from
God: the part God plays and the part you play. God is not
going to fail in doing His part. You know that. If you do
your part, you can be sure of an answer and the victory.

If you are defeated, you are defeated with your own
lips. You have defeated yourself. The Bible says in Proverbs 6:2, *"Thou art snared with the words of thy mouth."*
(Or, "Thou art taken captive with the words of thy
mouth.")

One writer put it this way: "You said that you could
not, and the moment you said it, you were whipped. You
said that you did not have faith, and doubt rose up like
a giant and bound you. You talked failure, and failure held
you in bondage."

If you talk about your trials, difficulties, lack of faith,

and lack of money — your faith will shrivel and dry up. But, bless God, if you talk about the Word of God, your lovely Heavenly Father and what He can do — your faith will grow by leaps and bounds.

If you confess sickness, it will develop sickness in your system. If you talk about your doubts and fears, they will grow and become stronger. If you confess lack of finances, it will stop the money from coming in. Although that may sound like a paradox, it is not. It is the truth. I have proven it true again and again.

Step 2: Do it.

Jesus dictated to me during my vision, *"Your action defeats you or puts you over. According to your action, you receive or you are kept from receiving."*

That is important! Let me state it again: Your action defeats you or puts you over. According to your action, you receive or you are kept from receiving.

This woman in Mark 5 had a number of obstacles to overcome. She did not pray that God would remove the obstacles; she just got up and walked over the top of them.

In Bible days, a woman with an issue of blood was regarded in the same category as a leper and was not to mix in public, according to the teaching of her religion. But her actions said, "Religion or no religion, I'm going to get my healing."

In that day, women did not have the privilege to mingle publicly. But again her actions said, "Custom or no custom, I'm going to get my healing."

When she got there, a multitude of people crowded between her and Jesus. In her weakened physical condition, that would have been enough to cause her to give up. But, blessed be God, her actions said, "Crowd or no crowd, I'm getting to Jesus," and she elbowed her way through.

This woman's actions showed her faith. Now get up and walk on top of the obstacles that have been standing between you and Jesus, and you and healing. Put *actions* as well as words with your faith.

It would not have done the woman with the issue of blood any good to have said, *"If I may touch but his clothes"* (v. 28) if she had not *acted* on what she said. She *did* it, praise God, and she received.

Step 3: Receive it.

Say it. Do it. Receive it.

"She felt in her body that she was healed of that plague" (v. 29).

Jesus said, "Virtue has gone out of me. Somebody has touched me" (v. 20). (Or as a marginal note reads, "He said, 'Power has gone out of me.' ")

I want you to notice something. Notice that the *feeling* and the *healing* followed the *coming* and the *doing.*

The woman *said* it first. She *came* for it second. Then she *received,* and *felt* in her body that she was healed. Most people want the feeling and the healing first, before the saying and the doing, but that's not how it works. You have to have the saying and action first. Then you will have the healing and feeling.

Jesus said, "Power has gone out of me." At that time, Jesus was the only representative of the Godhead at work on earth. He was anointed by the Holy Spirit. When He was on earth, if you wanted to go where the power was, you had to go where He was.

In Luke 5:17, the Bible says He was teaching on a certain day, and the Pharisees and doctors of the law from every town in Galilee and Judaea were gathered to hear him. *"And the power of the Lord was present to heal them."*

Jesus delegated a certain amount of that power to the 12 and sent them out, and He delegated a certain amount to the 70 and sent them out. Then, before He went away, He said, *"It is expedient for you that I go away: for if I go not away, the Comforter will not come unto you"* (John 16:7).

When Jesus returned to heaven, He sent the third Person of the Godhead, the Holy Spirit, to this earth. The Holy Spirit is the only Person of the Godhead at work on the earth today.

Now, as Jesus said to me, *"Power is always present everywhere."*

Oh, if people could only realize that! He is *everywhere!*

And wherever He is, there is power.

The whole world is concerned about radioactive material that is released when nuclear bombs are exploded in the atmosphere. This is a power that cannot be seen or felt, yet it is a power that is deadly and dangerous.

There is a power at work on the earth today that is neither deadly nor dangerous — a good power, a power that heals, delivers, and sets free. And this unseen, unheard power — this supernatural power — is always present everywhere.

It is like plugging into an electrical outlet. If we can learn how to plug into this supernatural power, we can put it to work for us, and we can be healed. *If every sick person in every sick room in the world just knew about this power and how to tap into it, it would heal them of every disease.*

If people in institutions only knew it, there is power

right there in that room where they are — more than enough power to heal them, to cure the insane, to drive out demons, and to deliver those who are bound.

If the power is there, you will ask, why isn't everyone healed? Let's return to this crowd where the sick woman pushed her way to Jesus.

"Daughter," Jesus said, *"THY FAITH hath made thee whole"* (v. 34). There is a secret here. It was *her faith* that caused that power to flow out to her. Jesus said to me, *"Power is always present everywhere"* — power to deliver from every sickness; power to deliver from every demon and everything that hurts or destroys. *Faith* gives it action.

Now we know the secret. It is not a hidden secret. It may be a secret to some, but it has been revealed to us and to all who will listen.

Jesus said, "Who touched me?" (v. 30), and the disciples replied, *"Thou seest the multitude thronging thee, and sayest thou, Who touched me?"* (v. 31).

Many people touched Jesus that day — some through curiosity, some accidentally, and some to see if something would happen. But no power flowed until there came a touch of faith! The minute there was a touch of faith, the power flowed out.

That day in 1934 when healing power enveloped my body and every symptom of distress, deficiency and physical wrongness was driven out of my body, I didn't realize what I was doing. I know now.

I simply acted on Mark 11:23,24. I began to say, "I believe God. I believe I receive healing for the deformed heart. I believe I receive healing for the paralysis. I believe I receive healing for the incurable blood disease." Those were the only three things the doctors had told me. In case I missed something, I said, "I believe I receive healing from the top of my head to the soles of my feet."

I knew I was acting on those Scriptures, and that is faith. Faith is acting on God's Word. Glory to God, I plugged into the power hose of heaven. I felt a warm glow strike me on the top of my head and ooze down over my body like somebody above me was pouring honey on me. It oozed over my head, down over my shoulders, down my arms, out to the ends of my fingers, and down my body. Feeling returned to the upper part of my body, where I had had perhaps 75 percent feeling. From my waist down, I felt nothing; I was dead. But when this power went down my body and out the ends of my toes, feeling returned, the paralysis disappeared, and I found myself standing in the middle of the room with my hands uplifted, praising God. I'm still healed now after more than 50 years.

Do you think God sent that healing power from heaven just that day? No! That power was in that room every day of those 16 months I was bedfast. Why didn't it do something? Because I hadn't turned the switch of faith on.

Many have died waiting for healing to come to them, saying, "I believe God is going to heal me *sometime.*" That is an unscriptural statement and contains no faith. It will not work.

People say, "Brother Hagin, do you know why the Lord won't heal me?"

Sometimes I shock them by replying, "God has already done all He is ever going to do about healing you."

Their eyes get big. "You mean He's *not* going to heal me?"

I tell them, "I didn't say that. I said that He has done

all He is ever going to do about healing you. You see, He sent Jesus to earth nearly 2,000 years ago, and He laid your sickness and your disease on Jesus, and Jesus bore them away. *'Himself took our infirmities, and bare our sicknesses'* (Matt. 8:17). God already has done something about your sicknesses. Why won't you accept what He has done?"

God is not *going* to do anything about it, because He already *has done* something about it. He has done something about salvation, the Holy Spirit, healing, and deliverance from demons. It is now up to you to plug in.

Faith is the plug, praise God. Just plug in.

How do you plug in?

Say it. Do it. Receive it.

Step 4: Tell it.

The woman *"came and fell down before him, and TOLD him all the truth"* (v. 33).

Not only Jesus, but the whole crowd, heard her. She *told* Him everything she had done.

Jesus said to me, "Tell it so others may believe."

You see, there is a difference between the first step (she *said* what she believed would happen) and the last step (she *told* what had happened).

Yes, it is scriptural to go tell it (Mark 5:19). Praise the Lord, He didn't say, "Go and debate the question of whether a person in your condition could be healed or not." He just said, "Go tell it."

In the vision, I said, "Lord, I can see that. I can see if anybody would take these four steps, they would receive healing just like that woman did.

"But now You said if anybody anywhere would take those four steps, they would receive from You *whatever*

they wanted. Do You mean that people can receive the infilling of the Holy Spirit that way?"

He said, "Most assuredly, yes."

Then I said to Him, "Lord, what about Christians? So
many believers need victory in various areas of their life.
They have the world, the flesh, and the devil to deal with.
Some need victory over the flesh. Some need victory over
the devil. Some need victory over the world. And some
need victory over all of it. Are You telling me that any
believer anywhere can write a ticket of victory over the
world, the flesh, and the devil? *They* can do it?"

He said emphatically, "Yes!"

He continued, "If they don't do it, it won't be done.
It would be a waste of their time to pray for Me to give
them the victory. They have to write their own ticket."

"But, Lord," I said, "You're going to have to give me
some Scripture to prove it. Your Word says, *'In the mouth
of two or three witnesses every word may be established'*
(Matt. 18:16). So give me more Scripture having these
same four principles in it, and I will believe it. I would not
accept any vision, even if I did see You, if You could not
prove what You said by the Bible."

No, He didn't reprimand me. He smiled and said, "All
right."

"There is a story from the Old Testament," He said,
"that you have known since you were a Sunday School
boy."

I couldn't think of any story that had these four principles in it, so I said, "You will have to tell me where it is."

He said, "In First Samuel, the 17th chapter, the story
of David and Goliath."

"Now wait a minute," I said. "You're not going to tell

me that is what David did?"

He said, "Exactly. Those are the four steps he took. The very first thing David did was *he said* " (v. 32).

You can read it for yourself. I read it after my vision. Five times David *said it* before he acted upon it.

David was sent by his father to take provisions to his brothers in the army and to find out how the war was progressing. When he got there, David found the Philistines encamped on one side of the valley, and the Israelites encamped on the other.

While David was there, a giant by the name of Goliath came out and challenged the armies of Israel, saying, "Send a man out against me. If I defeat him, you will be our servants, and if he defeats me, we will be your servants."

No man in Israel would go out against him, not even King Saul, who was head and shoulders taller than any man in Israel.

> 1 SAMUEL 17:32
> 32 AND DAVID SAID to Saul, Let no man's heart fail because of him; thy servant will go and fight with this Philistine.

And David said! Praise God, that's the first thing David did.

Here's a country boy, a teenager, who says he will go out and fight against the giant. His oldest brother, Eliab, had poked a little fun at his coming to the battlefield, saying, "Where are those sheep you're supposed to be watching?" Yet *David said:*

> 1 SAMUEL 17:34-37
> 34 AND DAVID SAID unto Saul, Thy servant kept his

father's sheep, and there came a lion, and a bear, and took
a lamb out of the flock:
35 And I went out after him, and smote him, and delivered
it out of his mouth: and when he arose against me, I caught
him by his beard, and smote him, and slew him.
36 Thy servant slew both the lion and the bear: and this
uncircumcised Philistine shall be as one of them, seeing he
hath defied the armies of the living God.
37 DAVID SAID MOREOVER, The Lord that delivered
me out of the paw of the lion, and out of the paw of the
bear, he will deliver me out of the hand of this Philistine.

David knew you can have what you say. He knew **you
can write your own ticket with God.** David is writing it
here. He knew God would do anything he would believe
Him for. God will do the same for you, too. The only reason
He has not done more for you is because you have not
believed Him for more!

In fact, *all you are and all you have today is the result
of what you believed and said in the past.*

Someone told Saul what David had said. He sent for
him.

Saul wanted to give David his armor, but David
wouldn't take it. *"And David said unto Saul, I cannot go
with these; for I have not proved them"* (v. 39).

David went out against Goliath armed only with his
shepherd's sling and staff. When the giant saw him, he
disdained David *"for he was but a youth, and ruddy."*
Goliath said, *"Am I a dog, that thou comest to me with
staves?"*

Goliath cursed David by his heathen gods and threatened
him. David let him talk. You can't stop the devil from talking. Let him blab. But when he gets through, you have
something to say.

AND DAVID SAID (he's still writing that ticket), *"Thou comest to me with a sword, and with a spear, and with a shield: but I come to thee in the name of the Lord of hosts, the God of the armies of Israel, whom thou hast defied"* (v. 45).

David is not through yet! David told Goliath, "I will feed your carcass and the carcasses of the host of the Philistines this day unto the fowls of the air, and to the wild beasts of the earth."

How could a teenage country boy say that? He was not a soldier. He had never been trained to fight. Yet here he is confronting a giant.

How tall was this giant? I did a little research. The Bible tells us that Goliath was six cubits and a span in height. According to the famous Jewish historian, Flavius Josephus, a cubit was measured differently at different times in Israel's history. If measured by the shorter length, Goliath was almost 10 feet tall. If measured by the longer length, Goliath was about 11 feet tall.

What did David do? David did not look at the situation from the standpoint of "how big I am" or "what I can do from the natural standpoint." He looked at it from the standpoint of "my God can do it."

David was measuring the giant by the size of God. It did not matter if Goliath were 11 feet tall. Compared to God, there is not even the resemblance of an ant to an elephant — not even the tiniest ant.

When you begin to measure your problems like this, your situation looks different. You see, "giants" look big when we measure ourselves by them.

You may be facing some of them today. I've faced them through the years. But when you put them beside God, they don't look big at all, because He's bigger. He's Bigger. He's BIGGER. He's GREATER! Greater is He that is in you than he that is in the world (1 John 4:4). Let's think in line with God's Word.

God is greater than the devil. He's greater than the giants that are in the land. He's greater than the enemy we face. He's greater than any power that can come against us. He's greater than any force that can be unleashed upon us.

When you think like that, when you look at things like that, when you believe and talk like that, sooner or later, you're going to arrive. David ran and hastened to meet the giant. He cut off the giant's head.

First, David *said* it. Second, he *did* it. Third, he *received* it. And fourth, they *told* it. The women got their tambourines and musical instruments and began to dance and sing, *"Saul has slain his thousands, but David his ten thousands"* (1 Sam. 18:7).

Some might wonder, "How did David know what God would do?"

He will do everything He said He would do, and He will do everything you believe Him for. **You can write your own ticket with God.**

Are you ready to write your ticket? If you need healing or victory over the world, the flesh, or the devil, say and act on God's Word, "I am writing a ticket of victory today."

You don't even have to have hands laid on you for healing.

People bound by habits like tobacco and dope have stood in front of me and said, "Brother Hagin, that thing left me, and I don't want it anymore." They wrote a ticket of victory. They said, "I've never been bothered by demons anymore." They took that giant's head off.

Don't measure yourself by the giant. Measure the giant by God.

Jesus said to me, "Israel is a type of the people of God. Goliath can be any giant that might be in your life: a type of the devil, demons, the world, the flesh, sickness, or anything else that stands between God's people and victory. Every child of God can write a ticket of victory."

In 1952, we were planning to hold a tent meeting in Clovis, New Mexico. When I told my mother about our proposed trip, she told me to drive carefully because "there are so many wrecks all the time."

She admitted that when I traveled, she stayed awake all night, praying, afraid a call would come saying I had been in a wreck. I told her that if she had been praying in faith, she could have gone to sleep. (I had to tell my own mother the truth just the same as anyone else.)

She said, "Son, I know you have faith. I never had much myself." (She was a member of a Full Gospel church, too, and she was talking herself right out of God's blessings.)

She said she knew I probably prayed every minute I was on the road.

I told her, "I never do. I never even pray that God will be with me."

"What makes you talk that way? What's gotten into you?" she said.

"Nothing but the Word," I told her. I reminded her that Jesus had already promised us, "*I will never leave thee nor forsake thee*" (Heb. 13:5). I told her I always start out by saying, "Heavenly Father, I'm so thankful for your

Word. I am so glad that Jesus is with me."

The 34th Psalm says, *"The angel of the Lord encampeth round about them that fear him, and delivereth them."* I told my mother that angels, as well as God, Jesus, and the Holy Spirit, are with me. I go singing and rejoicing.

Writing your own ticket with God, however, does not mean that things will fall on you like ripe cherries from a tree. You are not going to float through life on flowery beds of ease. The devil will try you and tempt you.

In 1954, after holding meetings in Oregon, we stopped in Salt Lake City to see the great Mormon Temple on the way home. As non-Mormons, we could not go inside, but a guide told us about the interior. He explained how the Mormons had transported the stones by ox cart and had built the temple to last for eternity.

On the spire of the temple is the likeness of an angel blowing a trumpet. This statue, of copper overlaid with gold leaf, is 12½ feet high. It is supposed to be the angel Moroni, who supposedly appeared to Joseph Smith in the 1820s and told him to dig up the gold plates from which Smith said he translated the Book of Mormon.

I cannot accept the Book of Mormon. I have read it, but it does not agree with the New Testament. As the Apostle Paul said, *"But though we, or an angel from heaven, preach any other gospel unto you than that which we have preached unto you, let him be accursed"* (Gal. 1:8).

As we stood there on the lawn listening to the guide, I heard someone behind me fall so hard his head popped up and hit again. A man said that a boy had fallen. The guide said, "That happens very often when I'm telling this story." He thought it was a supernatural sign to corrobo-

rate what he was telling. He said to drag the boy back
around the tree; he would come to in a minute.

I did not look back, but my wife did, and she said it
was our son, Ken Jr., who was 15 years old at the time.
He had hit the ground so hard that his shoes were kicked
off. His knees were drawn right up to his chest. His hands
were twisted, and his mouth was working in such convul-
sions that he was chewing his tongue. His eyes were set
and glazed.

Faster than machine gun bullets can fly, the devil shot
his darts into my mind and said, "You said that that
couldn't happen to your child." He gave me mental visions
of my son having epilepsy or some other kind of disease
and being in an institution while I was out preaching.

But, thank God, I knew how to write my ticket with
God.

I grabbed my son by the arms to lift him up. He was
stiff. I said, "Come out of him!" I had sensed evil spirits
when I walked on those grounds. I said, "I command you
to come out of him in the Name of the Lord Jesus Christ!"

Ken straightened out and blinked his eyes. He called
to me, and asked where he was and what had happened
to him. I told him that the devil had knocked him down,
but that Jesus was bigger than the devil. We wrote our
own ticket of victory.

The guide had said it was a supernatural manifestation verifying what he had said, but I got rid of his
manifestation with the Name of Jesus. You can say it and
do it.

You have authority over the devil. You don't need to
be defeated.

You can write your own ticket with God.
1. Say it.
2. Do it.
3. Receive it.
4. Tell it.

Chapter 7
The God-Kind of Faith

And on the morrow, when they were come
from Bethany, he was hungry:
And seeing a fig tree afar off having leaves,
he came, if haply he might find any thing
thereon: and when he came to it, he found
nothing but leaves; for the time of figs was not
yet.
And Jesus answered and said unto it, No man
eat fruit of thee hereafter for ever. And his
disciples heard it.
And in the morning, as they passed by, they
saw the fig tree dried up from the roots.
And Peter calling to remembrance saith unto
him, Master, behold, the fig tree which thou
cursedst is withered away.
And Jesus answering saith unto them, Have
faith in God.

— Mark 11:12-14; 20-22

Let us focus our attention on the statement, *"Have*
faith in God" (v. 22) or, as the margin reads, "Have the
faith of God." Greek scholars tell us this could have been
translated, "Have the God-kind of faith."

Jesus demonstrated that He had the "God-kind of
faith." From afar He saw that the fig tree had leaves, and
He approached it looking for fruit. Some have questioned
why Jesus looked for figs on this tree when it was not time
for them to be ripe. However, in that country those trees
which retained their leaves usually also had figs. Finding
no fruit on the tree, Jesus spoke to it, saying, *"No man*

eat fruit of thee hereafter for ever."

The next day when Jesus and His disciples passed by again, they found the tree dried up from the roots. Peter said, *"Master, behold, the fig tree which thou cursedst is withered away,"* which brought this amazing and startling statement from the lips of Jesus: *"Have faith in God* [have the faith of God, or the God-kind of faith]. *For verily I say unto you, That whosoever shall say unto this mountain, Be thou removed, and be thou cast into the sea; and shall not doubt in his heart, but shall believe that those things which he saith shall come to pass; he shall have whatsoever he saith"* (Mark 11:22,23).

After telling His disciples in verse 22 to have the God-kind of faith, Jesus went on to define and describe for us what it is. The God-kind of faith is the kind of faith in which a man: (1) believes in his heart, and (2) says with his mouth what he believes in his heart, and (3) it comes to pass.

Jesus showed that He had that kind of faith, for He believed that what He said would come to pass. He said to the tree, *"No man eat fruit of thee hereafter for ever." This is the kind of faith that spoke the world into existence!*

HEBREWS 11:3
3 Through faith we understand that the worlds were framed by the word of God, so that things which are seen were not made of things which do appear.

How did God do it? God believed that what He said would come to pass. He spoke the Word, and there was earth. He spoke into existence the vegetable kingdom. He spoke into existence the animal kingdom. He spoke into existence the heavens and the earth, the moon, the sun, the stars and the universe. He said it, and it was so. That is the God-kind of faith. *God believed what He said would come to pass, and it did!*

Jesus demonstrated that God-kind of faith to His disciples, and then He told them that they had that kind of faith — the faith in which a man believes with his heart, says with his mouth what he believes, and it comes to pass.

Someone might say, "I want that kind of faith. I am going to pray that God will give it to me." If you attempt this, you are wasting your time. You don't need to pray for it; you already have it.

ROMANS 12:3
3 For I say, through the grace given unto me, to every man that is among you, not to think of himself more highly than he ought to think; but to think soberly, according as God hath dealt to every man the measure of faith.

Every believer has been dealt a measure of the God-kind of faith. Paul wrote this to believers, for he says, "to every man that is among you." The Epistle to the Romans is not written to the sinners in the world; it is written to Christians. The letter is addressed to, *"all that be in Rome, beloved of God, called to be saints...."* (Rom. 1:7). And in this letter we are told that God has given to *"every man* [that is among you] *the measure of faith."* Every believer, every child of God, every Christian does have a measure of the God-kind of faith.

Further proof of this is seen in Ephesians 2:8, *"For by grace are ye saved through FAITH; and that not of yourselves: IT IS THE GIFT OF GOD."* The *faith* is not of yourself. He is not talking about the grace, for everyone

knows that grace is not of yourself. He is saying that the
faith by which you are saved is not of yourself. It is not
a natural human faith. It was given to sinners by God.
And how did God give the sinner faith to be saved?
Romans 10:17 says, *"So then faith cometh by hearing, and
hearing by the word of God."*

Notice the expressions we have just seen in regard to
faith: *"So then faith cometh...."* "God hath
dealt... faith." "Ye [are] saved through *faith;* and that not
of yourselves: *it is the gift...."*

Paul says that faith is *given,* it is *dealt,* it *cometh.*

ROMANS 10:8
8 But what saith it? The word is nigh thee, even in thy
mouth, and in thy heart: that is, the word of faith, which
we preach.

The Bible — this message of God — is called the Word
of faith. Why is it called the Word of faith? Because it
causes faith to come even into the heart of the unsaved.
It causes the kind of faith that spoke the universe into
existence to be dealt to our hearts. Faith is given to us
through the Word.

Notice again the words of Romans 10:8: "But what
saith it? The word is nigh thee, even *in thy mouth,* and
in thy heart: that is, the word of faith, which we preach."
This agrees exactly with the words of Jesus in Mark 11:23,
"Whosoever shall *say...* and shall not doubt in his
heart...."

We see here the basic principle inherent in the God-
kind of faith: believing it with the heart and saying it with
the mouth. Jesus believed it and He said it. God believed
it and He said it, speaking the earth into existence!

Verses nine and ten of this same tenth chapter of Romans say, "That if thou shalt *confess with thy mouth the Lord Jesus*, and shalt *believe in thine heart* that God hath raised him from the dead, thou shalt be saved. For *with the heart man believeth* unto righteousness; and *with the mouth confession* is made unto salvation."

A measure of faith is dealt to the sinner through hearing the Word. Then he uses it to create the reality of salvation in his own life.

When Christians are asked, "When were you saved?" they often answer by saying something like, "About nine on the night of July tenth." They are mistaken, however, because God saved them nearly 2,000 years ago. It became a reality to them only when they believed it and confessed it.

Salvation belongs to everyone. Every man and woman in this world has a legal right to salvation. Jesus died for the whole world, not just for you and me. When the truth is preached to the sinner, it causes faith to come. When he believes and confesses, he creates the reality of it in his own life by his faith.

ROMANS 10:13,14,17
13 For whosoever shall call upon the name of the Lord shall be saved.
14 How then shall they call on him in whom they have not believed? and how shall they believe in him of whom they have not heard? and how shall they hear without a preacher?
17 So then faith cometh by hearing, and hearing by the word of God.

Faith for salvation comes by hearing the Word of God. Faith for anything we receive from God comes in the same way. The God-kind of faith comes by hearing God's Word — and God has no kind of faith other than the God-kind. In other words, God gives or causes the God-kind of faith to come into the hearts of those who hear.

It is no wonder then that Jesus said, *"Take heed therefore how you hear"* (Luke 8:18). You cannot let it go in one ear and out the other, because that won't do any good. Faith won't come. If you act as if the Word of God were some fairy tale, faith will not come. But when you accept it reverently and sincerely, and act upon it, faith comes.

2 CORINTHIANS 4:13
13 We having the same spirit of faith, according as it is written, I believed, and therefore have I spoken; we also believe, and therefore speak.

We have the same spirit of faith. What belonged to the Church at Corinth belongs to the Church today. On no occasion did Paul or any of the apostles ever write to encourage the people to believe; never did they tell them to have faith. Our having to encourage believers to believe or have faith is a result of the Word of God's having lost its reality to us. We *are* believers!

When our children are away, we don't have to write to them and say, "Be sure to keep breathing." They will continue to breathe as long as they are alive. Neither do we have to encourage believers to believe, because that is what they are — believers.

How many of us realize that our words dominate us? *"Thou art snared with the words of thy mouth...."* (Prov. 6:2). Another version says, "Thou art taken captive with the words of thy mouth." One writer put it this way, "You

said you could not, and the moment you said it you were
defeated. You said you did not have faith, and doubt rose
up like a giant and bound you. You are imprisoned with
your own words. You talk failure, and failure holds you
in bondage.''

God created the universe with words. *Words filled with
faith are the most powerful things in all the world.*

Defeat and failure do not belong to the child of God.
God never made a failure. God made us new creatures. We
are not born of the will of the flesh or the will of man, but
the will of God. We are created in Christ Jesus. Failures
are man-made. They are made by wrong believing and
wrong thinking. First John 4:4 says, "...*Greater is he that
is in you, than he that is in the world.*" Learn to trust the
Greater One who is in you. He is mightier than anything
in the world.

The key to overcoming sickness and problems is the
God-kind of faith — believing with the heart and confess-
ing with the mouth. Our lips can make us victors or keep
us captives.

We can fill our words with faith or we can fill our words
with doubt.

We can fill our words with love that will melt the coldest
heart, or we can fill our words with hate and poison.

We can fill our words with love that will help the
discouraged and broken-hearted, and with faith that will
stir heaven.

We can make our words breathe the very atmosphere
of heaven.

Our faith will never rise above the words of our lips.
Jesus told the woman with the issue of blood that her faith
had made her whole. Thoughts may come and may persist

in staying. But if we refuse to put those thoughts into words, they die unborn. Cultivate the habit of thinking big things. Learn to use words that will react upon your own spirit. *Faith's confessions create realities.*

There are two things to notice about the God-kind of faith. First, a man believes in his heart. Second, he believes with his words. It is not enough to believe anything in your heart alone. To get God to work for you, you also have to believe with your words.

The unalterable law of faith is as Jesus said, "Whosoever shall *say* . . . and shall not doubt in his *heart,* but shall *believe* that those things which he *saith* shall come to pass; he shall have whatsoever he *saith* " (Mark 11:23).